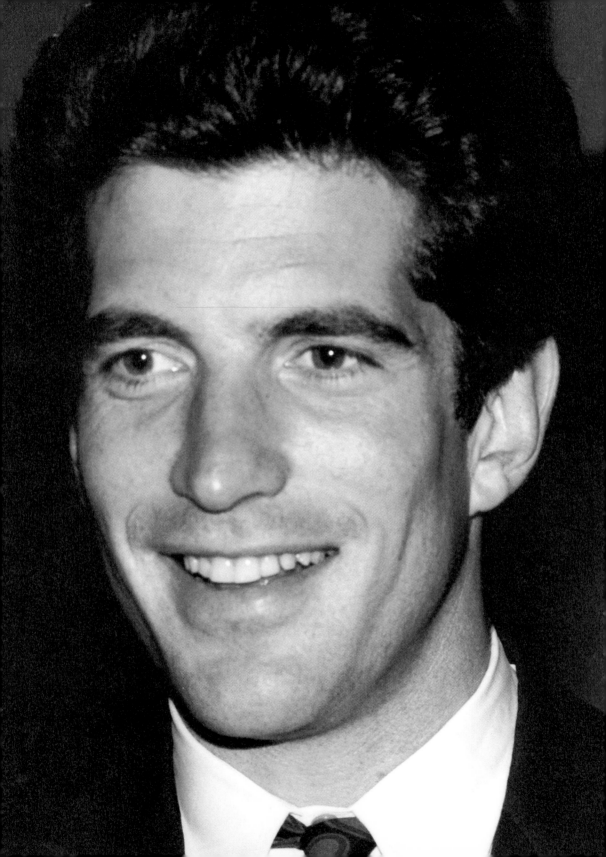

STEPHEN
SPIGNESI

A Citadel Press Book

**Published by
Carol Publishing Group**

A Citadel Press Book
Published by Carol Publishing Group
Citadel Press is a registered trademark of Carol Communications, Inc.

Editorial, sales and distribution, rights and permissions inquiries should be addressed to
Carol Publishing Group, 120 Enterprise Avenue, Secaucus, N.J. 07094

Carol Publishing books may be purchased in bulk at special discounts for sales promotion,
fund-raising, or educational purposes. Special editions can be created to specifications. For
details, contact Special Sales Department, 120 Enterprise Avenue, Secaucus, N.J. 07094

Manufactured in the United States of America

10 9 8 7 6 5 4 3 2

Library of Congress Cataloging-in-Publication Data

Spignesi, Stephen J.
        J.F.K. Jr. / Stephen Spignesi.
            p.   cm.
        "A Citadel Press book."
        ISBN 0-8065-1840-5 (pb)
        1. Kennedy, John F. (John Fitzgerald), 1960–1999 —Miscellanea.
2. Children of presidents—United States—Biography—Miscellanea.
3. Scrapbooks—United States. I. Title. II. Title: JFK Jr.
E843.K42S65 1996
973.922'092
[B]—DC20   96-41530
                                                             CIP

**Frontispiece: John Jr. is not a movie star, novelist, musician, politician, or athlete, and yet he
has fans.** PHOTO: PHOTOFEST

For Michele Stegmaier . . .

A good friend and publishing colleague whose courage and
good humor in the face of a few, ahem, "setbacks" has been
a continuing inspiration.

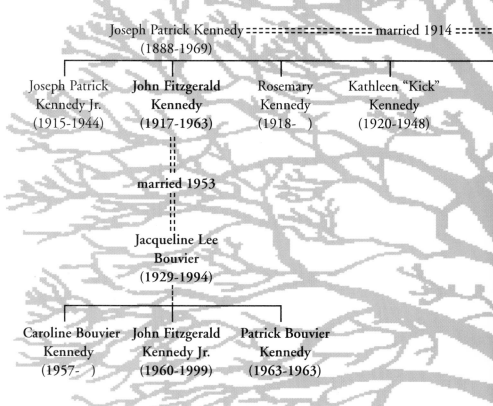

Joseph Patrick Kennedy ================ married 1914 ======
(1888-1969)

| Joseph Patrick Kennedy Jr. (1915-1944) | **John Fitzgerald Kennedy** **(1917-1963)** | Rosemary Kennedy (1918-   ) | Kathleen "Kick" Kennedy (1920-1948) |

married 1953

Jacqueline Lee Bouvier (1929-1994)

| Caroline Bouvier Kennedy (1957-   ) | John Fitzgerald Kennedy Jr. **(1960-1999)** | Patrick Bouvier Kennedy (1963-1963) |

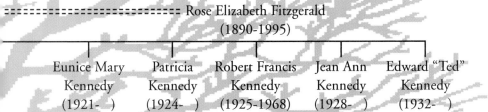

============================== Rose Elizabeth Fitzgerald
(1890-1995)

| Eunice Mary Kennedy (1921-) | Patricia Kennedy (1924-) | Robert Francis Kennedy (1925-1968) | Jean Ann Kennedy (1928-) | Edward "Ted" Kennedy (1932-) |

CONTENTS

This poignant moment is probably the most remembered photo of John Jr. that has ever been taken.
PHOTO: PHOTOFEST

ACKNOWLEDGMENTS

Many thanks to . . .

My editor, Michael Lewis, for his inspired suggestions and guidance;

My previous editor Marcy Swingle, for her, shall we say, unbridled passion for this project in its early days;

My publisher, Steven Schragis, for his sustaining encouragement and for keeping me busy;

My agent and *meraviglioso sostenitore* John White, for service above and beyond;

My friends Ron Mandelbaum and Howard Mandelbaum at Photofest;

The fine folks at Sotheby's, Journal Graphics, the University of New Haven Library, The Hagaman Memorial Library in East Haven, CT;

Tommy K's in Branford, CT;

The "stellar" Paul Levatino;

The "picturesque" AnnMarie Levatino;

My Big Apple copilot, Frank Mandato;

and, of course . . .

Pam, Lee Mandato, Michele Stegmaier, and Linda Beavis.

Here comes the son! This photo was taken at a 1963 Veteran's Day observance at the Tomb of the Unknowns eleven days before President Kennedy was assassinated. PHOTO: PHOTOFEST

INTRODUCTION: HERE COMES THE SON

Winter is an ugly season.

Sure, it's pretty for the first forty-two seconds or so when the snow is first falling. But then it isn't long before the dogs dye the snow yellow and the road crews stain it brown and what was once pristine white has been transformed into a blanket of cold, ugly filth.

Nevertheless, there are always islands of beauty and charm in any desolate landscape and for many, many women, no matter what it looks like outside, the visage of John F. Kennedy Jr. unfailingly brightens and warms their frostbitten and depressed winter hearts.

While I was working on *J. F. K. Jr.*, I was amazed at the reaction I got from women when I told them about the book's subject. John F. Kennedy Jr. turns otherwise politically correct women into raging sexists. Men seem to be immune, but women? No way. Women (and this is not a sexist generalization but rather a firsthand observation) perceptibly swooned when John Jr.'s name was mentioned. And I'm talking about females from the ages of eighteen to eighty: They all felt it necessary to remind me that John Jr. was "gorgeous," "magnificent," and to ask me if I could help them out with a home phone or address. John Jr. has that effect on women.

Who is being spoken of here?

Few if any Americans have been born with [such] advantages: a famous name; a brilliant father who labored unceasingly to develop his son's natural talents; and an extraordinary mother.

This sounds like John F. Kennedy Jr., doesn't it?

He has the "famous name," the "brilliant father" devoted to helping his son be the best he can be, and, let's face it, if there was ever a word to describe Jacqueline Kennedy Onassis, "extraordinary" is it.

But no, the cited passage was not written to describe John Jr. The quoted excerpt was written by his *father*, President Kennedy, in his book *Profiles in*

Courage, to describe the sixth President of the United States, John Quincy Adams.

I first came across this quote while listening to an audiotape reading of *Profiles in Courage* . . . read by John F. Kennedy Jr.

One has to wonder if John Jr., as he was reading that passage, recognized the undeniable historical (and personal) parallels in those words.

John F. Kennedy Jr. is not a movie star, a novelist, a musician, a politician, or an athlete, and yet he has *fans*.

The United States is not a monarchy and yet the prevailing perception of John F. Kennedy Jr. is that he is a part of American royalty.

Our country tends to become obsessed with achievers and doers. In many ways, the United States is a genuine free market meritocracy, and we gladly lavish wealth and fame on those who make it *big*. We love winners. John F. Kennedy Jr. is only just beginning to make his name in the world of business, and yet for the past thirty years we have almost blinded the poor guy with the repeated explosions of flashbulbs every time he appears in public.

We know the names of his girlfriends; what he eats for breakfast; how much money he makes; and his private test scores are plastered on the front pages of the New York tabloids as though he was an Olympic runner whose latest times we absolutely *have to know*.

His birth made headlines around the world, and he broke our hearts when he saluted his slain father's coffin at the age of three.

He is breathtakingly handsome, impeccably poised, and he handles the press with such good-natured aplomb that even the most jaded of journalists run out of superlatives when describing him.

What must it be like to have the world fixate on and obsess over your love life?

Do you think John F. Kennedy Jr. gets out of bed every morning, looks in his bathroom mirror, and sees "John F. Kennedy Jr."?

Silly question, I know, but the point of it is that John's history and family have transcended normal life and turned him into something akin to an unreal character in a play called *America's History*.

J. F. K. Jr. is for all those who are passionate about John F. Kennedy Jr. and also for those who are merely interested in the life and times of America's favorite son.

J. F. K. Jr. is an intimate look at the heir to Camelot, and at the sexiest of all Kennedys; a man who many think may someday be President of the United States. After all, he is the rightful heir, isn't he?

Why did John and Daryl Hannah break up?

How did John feel about initially flunking the bar exam?

What kind of relationship does John have with his sister Caroline?

What's the truth about the secret nude photos of John?

Does John ever want to get into politics and if so, will he ever run for President?

Has John ever seen Oliver Stone's movie about his father's assassination?

What is John's favorite vegetable?

What was his and Carolyn's wedding song?

These and countless other questions are all answered in *J. F. K. Jr.*, a look at a young man who is a reluctant idol to many; and an undeniable living symbol of a part of America's history that his mother called Camelot.

John at the Special Olympics in 1995 in New Haven, Connecticut. John's aunt Eunice Shriver founded the organization and John has always been a staunch supporter.
PHOTO: ANNMARIE LEVATINO

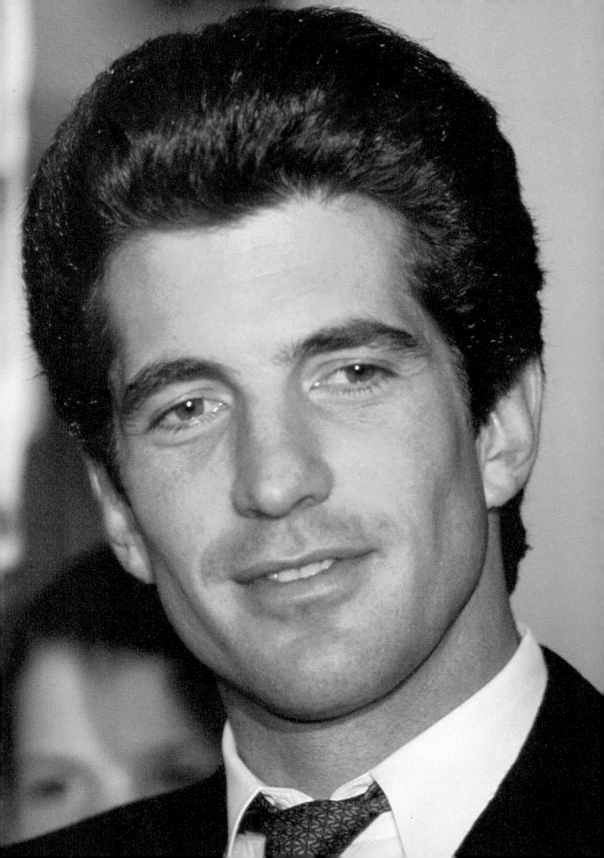

THE LIFE AND TIMES OF JOHN F. KENNEDY JR.

My son—and what's a son? A thing begot

Within a pair of minutes, thereabout,

A lump bred up in darkness.

—THOMAS KYD, *Additions*

Photogenesis

The life of John F. Kennedy Jr. has been like a quicksilver succession of photographic images, all of which are indelibly etched into the collective consciousness of America.

We all have seen the photo of John as a two-year-old infant crawling around under the big wooden desk of his father, the President; and we have all also seen—countless times—three-year-old John saluting the coffin of his slain father. From there, the images blur into one long succession of pictures of John as a young boy, as a gangly teen (with a huge halo of curly hair), and into later views of John as the handsome young man one woman writer I know described as an "Adonis."

America has watched John grow up; we've followed him through his school years; into college; on his travels; through law school; and, of course (much to John's chagrin), we've been along on many of his dates. And even though his political involvement has been extremely limited, there exists in this country a perception that we are simply biding our time; patiently waiting until John is ready to run for public office.

John is the hesitant heir to Camelot. The kingdom would seem to be his for the taking—if he ever decides he wants it.

The President Has a Son

John F. Kennedy and Jacqueline Bouvier Kennedy were married on Saturday, September 12, 1953. Their first child, Caroline, was born in 1957.

J.F.K. Jr. for President in 2008? Talk about name recognition, eh? Stay tuned for future developments in the life and times of John F. Kennedy Jr.! PHOTO: BROOKS KRAFT, SYGMA

There is a possibly apocryphal (yet oft-repeated) story about how Jackie conceived John, Jr. Seven years after their wedding, the story goes, on February 15, 1960 (after Jackie had already had one miscarriage), Jackie shook hands with a minister's wife who had had thirteen children. J.F.K. reportedly had told his wife, "Shake hands with this lady, Jackie. Maybe it will rub off on you." Eight months later, on November 25, 1960, (seventeen days early), John was born. (His original due date was December 12, 1960.)

The Early Years

After John's premature birth, Jackie stayed in father-in-law Joseph Kennedy's Palm Beach house with the children's nanny, Maud Shaw, until returning to Washington in January 1961 for J.F.K.'s inauguration. (Jackie and the children moved to Washington permanently in late February 1961.)

John's nurse for the first three months of his life was a British woman named Elsie Phillips, a friend of Miss Shaw's.

Nanny Shaw felt that John was a little underweight when they moved to the White House from the Palm Beach house in February 1961 and she often fed him beef extract for lunch in order to strengthen him and help him gain weight.

When John was only a couple of days old, Miss Shaw took Caroline to a store so she could buy her new brother a present. She picked out a silver comb and brush set.

John's nursery in the White House was an exceptionally large room decorated in blue and white. The room boasted a gas stove on which his nanny prepared John's formulas. When Caroline was only three years old, she would help her mother and Miss Shaw by giving John his bottle.

Infant John got his morning bottle at six A.M. and took his morning nap in a carriage on the Truman Balcony (the balcony President Truman added to the White House). He inherited his sister Caroline's crib, which was redecorated with blue bows instead of Caroline's pink ones.

The White House

Jackie established a kindergarten in the third floor solarium of the White House. (This was the room where President Eisenhower regularly sat in the sun.) Twelve to fifteen children attended this unique schoolroom, mostly the children of friends of the Kennedys and children of embassy personnel. Caroline did very well during her time in this class, but John never attended. (He often, however, joined the children for morning recess when he grew old enough to run and play.) The school closed abruptly after President Kennedy's death and then moved to the British embassy.

As a child of three, John could completely dress himself. He only needed help with his buttons and shoes.

John was always fascinated by the Revolutionary War wallpaper in the First Family's second floor White House dining room. The paper had come from a house Jackie had heard about that was being demolished. She had the colorful paper carefully removed from the walls before the house was torn down.

The President has a son, and there are babies in the White House for the first time in nearly 70 years. A well-bundled John was just over two months old when this picture was taken.
PHOTO: PHOTOFEST

As a child, John liked to set up his own little kitchen in the corner of the White House kitchen, using pots and pans and other paraphernalia. The White House chefs and maids would play right along with him.

When they were children, only the toys and gifts given to John and Caroline by closest friends and family members were accepted. All the rest (and there were many) were donated to the Kennedy Foundation Hospital for Children.

As a three year old, John once took a fancy to one of Caroline's toys, a grey donkey on wheels named Neddie. Caroline gladly gave John the donkey.

John once dropped a toy gun off the White House balcony just prior to a speech by Marshall Tito of Yugoslavia. The falling gun was caught on film and the media inserted the clip into coverage of Tito's speech, making it appear as though John had been playing on the balcony throughout the speech. John's nanny had actually taken John to Dumbarton Oaks for a walk, leaving the White House fifteen minutes prior to the speech. J.F.K. queried Miss Shaw about the incident but accepted her explanation. Little John had nearly caused an international incident!

John lost one of his front teeth when he banged into the corner of a step on which he fell while playing in a big doll house on the White House lawn. His doctors did not put the tooth back because of the fear of tetanus.

As a child, it took John a while to be able to pronounce his sister Caroline's name. For some time the closest he could come was "Cannon." (Caroline used to translate John's baby talk for their father.)

John and Caroline regularly joined their father in the White House pool for his evening swim.

Caroline and John had their own three-man Secret Service detail when they lived in the White House: The Secret Service detail consisted of Lynn Meredith (head of the unit), Bob Foster, and Tom Wells. When Caroline and

Nanny Maud Shaw cared for John and Caroline as if they were her own. Here she leads them to a plane at Andrews Air Force Base for a 1962 trip to the Kennedy compound in Palm Beach, Florida.
PHOTO: PHOTOFEST

John were children, Nanny Shaw insisted that they address their Secret Service agents as "Mister," rather than by the agent's first names (which the agents themselves had suggested). Whenever Caroline and John left the White House grounds, there was always one Secret Service agent in the car with them and their nanny, and two more agents in a tail car behind them.

John was taught to ride a bike by his Secret Service agent Bob Foster and he quickly learned that he could get anything he wanted (including forbidden candy before lunch) just by asking one of his Secret Service agents.

As children, bedtime was bedtime for John and Caroline: They never gave their parents or their nanny any trouble about going to bed.

In her book, Miss Shaw relates that John liked to tell his nanny that he was her "big boy" when he had been "good or specially clever." According to Miss Shaw, "John loved to be thought of as a big boy."

John liked to try and keep up with his sister's "riddling." He would do so by asking his nanny ridiculous questions and then providing non sequitur answers. He would then laugh hilariously at his extremely clever "riddles."

Jackie and J.F.K. would occasionally argue over the length of John's hair. Jackie wanted to let John's hair grow long, "European" style; while his father favored it shorter. When J.F.K. saw that John's hair was getting longer and longer, he one day good-naturedly gave Miss Shaw a "Presidential Order" to give his son a haircut. As a toddler, John *hated* having his hair cut and his nails trimmed.

John enjoyed building sand castles and then demolishing them "with ferocious gusto."

John did not like horses or horseback riding.

As children, John and Caroline were allowed to pick the menu when they had picnics at Egg Island off Hyannis. According to Nanny Shaw, their "menu" inevitably "tended to be comprised of huge quantities of ice cream, fruit and cakes."

As a child, John was a "complete extrovert," according to his nanny. This is an interesting observation when one considers the many acquaintances of John Jr. who claim that as an adult he is a serious exhibitionist, often walking around half-naked, or, as when he visited a nude beach, *completely* naked. (See Chapter 6, the "Scandals" chapter, for more details on nude photos of John from that beach outing.)

During miniature golf games, John would get upset and storm off the green, exclaiming to his nanny, "The ball never goes where I hit it, Miss Shaw!"

One year, John gave his mother an especially "artistic" gift: He covered a big sheet of paper with paint and "signed" his name at the bottom. John also once painted a portrait of his nanny, except to Miss Shaw, it looked like a drawing of the beach. "It's not the beach," John informed her with earnest dignity. "It's you."

According to Miss Shaw, neither John nor Caroline were "bratty" or spoiled.

John liked to sit behind the controls of the White House helicopter. He would wear a helmet and pretend he was taking off and flying it. He would make all the correct noises and insisted on being called "Captain John." He would issue orders to J.F.K., who would, of course, comply.

Interestingly, when Jackie and J.F.K. flew off in the helicopter on the morning of their fateful trip to Dallas, John did not cry as he stood there waving them off. Nanny Shaw remembers this as the very first time he didn't cry when watching his parents fly off and leave him behind.

Jackie and John head for John's very first church service at St. Stephen's Church in Middleburg, Virginia in 1962.
PHOTO: PHOTOFEST

The Assassination

The assassination of John's father may well be one of the most significantly defining moments of the twentieth century. No other historical event has generated the huge amount of speculation, controversy, and study as that day in Dallas. Throughout his life, John has had to endure ongoing discussion and dissection of a terrible personal family tragedy.

To his credit, John has never discussed the myriad Kennedy assassination theories or become part of the subculture that has evolved surrounding the murder of his father.

The author remembers reading an interview with John in which he was asked if he had seen Oliver Stone's movie *JFK* and, when he replied that he had not, was then asked why he hadn't. John movingly explained that repeatedly watching his father get shot was not his idea of entertainment and, with that response, spoke volumes about his own feelings about the assassination. It made us all realize that J.F.K. was his *father*, and that even though the martyred President has become what can only be described as a mythological creature (much the way many other members of his family are perceived, but none more so than J.F.K. and Jackie) in American history, to John and Caroline, he was, quite simply, their dad.

John was told about his father's assassination by his uncle, Robert Kennedy (then U.S. Attorney General).

John and Caroline watched the private funeral mass for their father through the open doors of the White House Green Room.

President Kennedy was buried on Monday, November 25, 1963, John's third birthday, and according to Miss Shaw, John became after his father's death "as restless as his father had been." The slain President was interred with a miniature flag that John picked out from a board at the Capitol which was decorated with flags of all nations. He asked, "Please, may I have one for Daddy?"

As she recounted in her book, at J.F.K.'s funeral, Miss Shaw had to chase a rather rambunctious John and bring him back to the nursery. As she was leading him back, England's Prince Philip saw her and said, "I've got one like that. They're a handful, aren't they?," to which Miss Shaw offhandedly replied, "Heavens, you're right." It wasn't until later that she realized with whom she had casually chatted.

On the night after the assassination, Jackie, Caroline, and John (and nanny Shaw) temporarily moved into Averill Harriman's house on N Street in Washington, D.C. John, at three years old, was a little put out that he had to climb three flights of stairs up to his bedroom. The White House had had an elevator.

Aftermath

John brought with him to this temporary home his guns, swords, and a few mechanical toys. He also brought his Marine uniform, which he insisted on wearing almost all the time.

After his father's death, John received a construction set as a gift. He loved playing with it and would build houses and forts with the small tiles.

Eventually Jackie bought a house in Washington at 3017 N Street. People used to gather outside the N street house, hoping to catch a glimpse of Jackie and the children. This quickly got annoying. The children simply could not understand why people wanted to take their picture.

As the days passed, John would sometimes ask his mother why they weren't still living in the "other house."

New York

In January 1964, John caught chicken pox from his sister.

In September of that year, in an effort to get away from the glare of the spotlight they were under in Washington, Jackie moved her family to New York City, taking an apartment in the Carlyle Hotel for six weeks while their new home at 1040 Fifth Avenue was readied.

Jackie felt that New York was a place where her children could be "left in peace" and where they could "rehabilitate" themselves after J.F.K.'s tragic death.

Every Christmas, a pastry chef would send Caroline and John a beautiful gingerbread house as a Christmas gift. One year, the chef and his assistant came to the Fifth Avenue apartment, requesting that their picture be taken with the children. Nanny Shaw refused their request but when Jackie heard that the men who so thoughtfully sent her kids such a beautiful gift were downstairs, she allowed the photo to be taken.

To escape the spotlight following J.F.K.'s assassination, Jackie moved to New York in 1964. This is the first posed picture of Jackie and John Jr. taken in her new office. Notice the books about the White House in the bookcase behind her. PHOTO: PHOTOFEST

School Days

In New York, John attended St. David's School in Manhattan from 1965 to 1968; then the Collegiate School for Boys in Manhattan from 1968 to 1976. As a teenager, he attended Phillips Academy in Andover, Massachusetts from 1976 to 1979; and then went on to Brown University in Providence, Rhode Island from 1979 to 1983, where he earned a Bachelor's Degree in History.

John also attended the University of Delhi in New Delhi, India in 1985. He did not earn a degree there but took courses in health care, food production, and adult education. After a three-year hiatus, John attended New York University Law School in Manhattan from 1986 to 1989, earning a Law Degree. He passed the New York State Bar exam after his third try in July 1990.

Aristotle Onassis

On Sunday, October 20, 1968, at 5:15 p.m., nearly five years after President Kennedy had been shot, John's mother Jackie married Greek businessman Aristotle Onassis. The marriage took place only after the finalizing of a prenuptial agreement that one Jackie biographer described as being more like a bill of sale for a person than a financial agreement.

Jackie, John, and Aristotle Onassis at the third game of the 1969 World Series.
PHOTO: PHOTOFEST

John was eight years old when his mother married Onassis. It is generally believed that the assassination of her brother-in-law Robert Kennedy spurred her to agree to the marriage. She was widely quoted as saying, "If they're killing Kennedys, then my children are targets." She believed that Onassis's wealth and lush hideaways all over the world (including his own island) would provide her and her children with the security and privacy she so desperately sought.

John related quite well to his stepfather Aristotle Onassis, and Ari told John they were *filaracos*, which means "buddies" in Greek. Jackie was pleased with this development because she earnestly wanted her son to have a male role model. They became good friends, and Ari did with John the "male" things his father and uncle would have done if they had lived.

Jackie's marriage to Onassis afforded John and Caroline with an unimaginably wealthy, jet set lifestyle that included summer travel to places like Paris and

Montevideo, but that unfortunately also gave Jackie a worldwide reputation as a golddigger. A British tabloid went so far as to run the headline, "Jackie Weds Blank Check," and the outcry around the world was blisteringly critical of Jackie.

Jackie, being the woman that she was, however, ignored the criticism and never discussed her marriage publicly.

In 1975, after seven years of marriage, Onassis died from bronchial pneumonia, leaving John the trifling sum of $25,000 in his will. Jackie would have none of that, however, and she renegotiated the will with Onassis's daughter Christina, ultimately agreeing to a $26 million settlement. This gave Jackie and her family financial security for life and reportedly made Caroline and John millionaires by the time they each turned twenty-one.

The profile that makes many admirers' hearts beat a little faster!
PHOTO: PHOTOFEST

For the next decade or so, John attended school and dutifully appeared at Kennedy family functions where he was often photographed with his many cousins. From many accounts, he tried to lead as normal a life as he could during his high school and college years. This was not always possible, however, since the press and the paparazzi relentlessly followed his every move and photographed him whenever he was out in public. To his credit, though, John maintained a good-natured rapport with the press during these years and never lost his cool or exploded in anger.

The Man

Workin' for a Livin': In 1984, after his graduation from Brown, John took his first paying job at the age of twenty-four. He was the assistant to the New York Commissioner of Business Development and he earned $20,000 a year. By this time, John was a millionaire several times over. There were many photos and reports of John arriving for work on his bicycle wearing shorts and a T-shirt. He changed when he got to work and then changed back into biking clothes for the ride home.

In 1987, during his summer vacation from law school, John worked as a law clerk in the civil rights division at the U.S. Justice Department. He earned $353 a week. His time in Washington was relatively uneventful and it was reported that instead of power lunches at fancy restaurants, John spent most of his lunch hours brown-bagging it in his office.

In 1988, again during his summer vacation from law school, John took a job at the Los Angeles law firm of Manatt, Phelps, Rothenberg, and Phillips. He earned $1,100 a week. Charles Manatt, one of the founders of this law

John backstage at the 1995 Special Olympics. PHOTO: ANNMARIE LEVATINO

firm was John's uncle Ted Kennedy's law school roommate. One of the attorneys at the firm was quoted as saying that John was no prima donna: He worked on "anything he was given."

After law school, John took a job as an assistant district attorney at the Manhattan Criminal Courts Building. He was one of sixty-nine new DAs who started work in August 1989. His starting salary was $29,999 a year and he worked there for three years before leaving in July 1993. In his four years with the NYC District Attorney's office John prosecuted five cases and won them all.

John then spent the next several months vacationing and developing his magazine, *George*, which debuted in September 1995. John's official title is Editor-in-Chief and Co-Founder. John writes an "Editor's Letter" every month and also personally conducts a high-profile interview each month. Beginning with the June/July 1996 issue, the magazine began billing John's talk as "The John Kennedy Interview."

To Be Continued . . .

Today, John is newly married to Carolyn Bessette and they live in his TriBeCa (New York City) loft. There are persistent rumors that she is pregnant but, of course, John and Carolyn do not talk to the press and do not give credence to media stories by responding to them in any way at all.

John has expressed a sincere commitment to his fledgling magazine, *George*, which is holding its own in a volatile and extremely competitive climate, and which has provided John with his most public role to date. He personally introduced the magazine at a press conference in September of 1995, telling the assembled media, "I don't think that I have seen as many of you in one place since they announced the results of my first bar exams." He also mentioned his father at the press conference, one of the rare times he has spoken of the senior J.F.K. in public:

> *In a moment of anger, my father once said that all businessmen are s.o.b.'s and I have to admit that more than once during this process I couldn't have agreed with him more. That feeling has passed, and now I am one of them.*

John has not expressed any interest in running for office, but one political pundit suggests the possibility that if John ever did decide to enter the "family business," he would skip the local and state races, and run as the Democratic candidate for President in 2004 or 2008. That remains to be seen.

In the meantime, though, we will continue to watch John as he plays Frisbee in Central Park, and flies all over the world for business trips and vacations.

John F. Kennedy Jr., the only son of a slain President, is still a young man, and the road lies long before him.

(ALMOST) EVERYTHING YOU'VE ALWAYS WANTED TO KNOW ABOUT JOHN F. KENNEDY JR.

This feature is a potpourri of interesting, intriguing, funny, and just plain useless information about America's favorite son.

■ John Fitzgerald Kennedy Jr. was born at Georgetown University Hospital in Washington, D.C. early on Friday morning, November 25, 1960. He was the first child ever born to a President-elect, (and the first baby in the White House since 1893, the year President Grover Cleveland's daughter Esther was born there). His parents were John F. Kennedy, who had just been elected the thirty-fifth President of the United States (and who was assassinated Friday, November 22, 1963); and Jacqueline Bouvier Kennedy Onassis (who died Thursday, May 19, 1994).

■ John was delivered by cesarean section seventeen days earlier than his due date of December 12. He was born with hyaline membrane disease, a respiratory disorder that required that he spend his first five days in an incubator. Hyaline membrane disease was a mild form of the condition that three years later, would kill his infant brother, Patrick Kennedy.

■ John weighed 6 pounds, 3 ounces at birth. (John was smaller at birth than his sister Caroline who weighed in at 7 pounds, 2 ounces. When Caroline was born, President Kennedy described her as looking "as robust as a sumo wrestler.")

■ John's birth raised the population of the United States to 182,000,267.

■ When John was born, the Internal Revenue Service issued a press release announcing that J.F.K. and Jackie could now take an additional six hundred dollar deduction on their 1960 tax return.

■ After John Jr. was born, thousands of Americans named their newborn children John, Caroline, and Jacqueline.

■ John was baptized on Friday, December 9, 1960, in the chapel at Georgetown University Hospital. On that same day Jackie was given a welcoming tour of the White House by Mamie Eisenhower.

■ According to John and Caroline's childhood nanny, Miss Maud Shaw, both John and President Kennedy preferred mechanical playthings over spend-

"What a son!" Here John sports a look that has convinced many he could have been a model if he had so chosen. PHOTO: GERARDO SOMOZA, OUTLINE

ing time with animals. This is a surprise considering that during their childhood years, the First Family owned (and visited, in the case of a snake named George) the following pets:

A Welsh terrier named Charlie.

A Cocker Spaniel named Shannon, a gift from President Eamin De Valera of Ireland.

An Irish Wolfhound referred to as both Wolfie and Wolf, a gift from a priest in Dublin.

The day of John's christening. John wore the same christening gown his father had worn 43 years earlier.
PHOTO: PHOTOFEST

A German Shepherd named Clipper, a gift from Joseph Kennedy.

Two hamsters named Marybell and Bluebell, one of whom died in J.F.K.'s bathtub.

A puppy named Pushinka, a gift from Kruschev.

A beer-drinking rabbit named Zsa Zsa that could play the trumpet.

A kitten named Tom Kitten, aka Tom Terrific.

Two canaries, one of whom was named Robin.

Two parakeets.

Two ponies named Macaroni and Leprechaun.

Two deer, both of which were given to the New York Children's Zoo. John was later amazed by the fact that the two deer he saw in the zoo were the ones he and Caroline had had at the White House: "They are *our* deer, aren't they, Miss Shaw?" he would ask their nanny.

An Indian tiger cub and an Indian elephant, presented to the children. Both were not accepted by Jackie.

A cobra named George(!) who lived at a snake farm Caroline and John loved to visit when the First Family drove to Camp David. They would let him crawl all over them.

■ When John was five years old, if asked his name, he would offer his hand to shake and answer, "I'm John F. Kennedy Jr."

The "John–John" Myth Jackie and J.F.K.'s childhood nickname for John was NEVER John–John. Jackie called him "Johnny"; his father called him "John." Secret Service agent Dave Powers explained to Jackie biographer Lester David the genesis of that story:

One day Jack was trying to get John's attention and he called his name, clapping his hands at the same time. When the child did not respond, Jack clapped again and called, "John, John." Somebody in the press overheard and it was "John–John" after that.

■ Throughout his childhood (and, of course, into adulthood), John *hated* (and still hates) being called "John–John."

■ After their father's assassination, John and Caroline wanted to know two things: Caroline wanted to know if their brother Patrick would be watching out for their daddy in heaven. John, ever the pragmatist, wanted to know if there was fish chowder in heaven. Fish chowder had been one of his daddy's favorite dishes and the family assured him that he was having it whenever he wanted it.

■ According to his nanny, Maud Shaw, at the age of four, John was interested in "cowboys and Indians, guns, swords, soldiers, airplanes, and space rockets." She also described him as "bloodthirsty" and told the story of John's visit to a children's theater during which he kept asking when the character with the axe would "chop someone's head off." No one ended up losing their head and John groused about it all the way home. Also as a child, John used to play air guitar and sing The Beatles' "She Loves You" for his mother, and Miss Shaw. He loved to watch the lions get fed at the Bronx Zoo.

■ One of the most famous photographs of John during the White House years shows him playing underneath his father's desk in the Oval Office. Today, President Bill Clinton uses the same desk in the Oval Office. This desk was made from wood from the sailing ship Resolute. Shortly after moving in, Jackie found the desk hidden away in the White House and had it installed in the Oval Office.

■ Jackie refused to allow White House photographers to take pictures of John's bedroom. She is quoted as saying, "Gentlemen, even at the age of two, one's bedroom should be private."

■ When John, his mother, and Caroline left the White House for the last time in 1963, he was carrying his father's posthumously-awarded Presidential Medal of Freedom.

■ When John was six, he caused a ruckus at the wedding of Janet Auchincloss by trying to make ponies run through the reception tent.

■ When John was seven, he collected scrimshaw.

■ After J.F.K.'s assassination, Jackie reacted to the relentless attention given to her children by admitting "We would never even have named John after his father if we had known . . ."

John is nearly four as he takes his first steps on skis on Mt. Mansfield in Stowe, Vermont, in March of 1964. Mom Jackie lends a guiding hand.
PHOTO: PHOTOFEST

■ In 1968, President Johnson dedicated the East Garden of the White House to Jackie. Instead of attending the ceremony herself, however, Jackie sent her mother in her place. Lyndon and Lady Bird Johnson were terribly offended by this insult and in an attempt to apologize, Jackie sent them three crayon drawings done by John Jr. It didn't work.

■ When John was a child, his grandmother Rose Kennedy would test him to make sure he knew all his prayers.

■ Jackie sent John to New York psychiatrist Dr. Ted Becker during his time at Collegiate because she believed he could get better grades. (He was only getting average grades and this was not acceptable to Jackie.)

John, Caroline, and Jackie in 1966 during a visit to a friend's cattle ranch in Cordoba, Argentina. Jackie and Caroline watch attentively as John sheaths his mighty (toy) sword.
PHOTO: PHOTOFEST

■ John's Secret Service code name when he attended St. David's School was "Lark."

■ Some of John's St. David's classmates were terribly cruel to him, following him and shouting, "Your father's dead! Your father's dead!" John turned to his mother for comfort.

■ When John's St. David's teachers wanted him to repeat the first grade because they felt he was too immature to move ahead, Jackie transferred him to the Collegiate School—and enrolled him in the second grade.

■ When John attended Collegiate, he took the bus to school—followed by an unmarked car filled with Secret Service agents.

■ As an adult, John is 6 feet, 1 inch tall and his weight fluctuates between 175 and 190 pounds.

■ John and his cousin William Kennedy Smith attended St. David's School together. During summer vacations in Hyannis Port, Massachusetts, John's clique of Kennedy cousins consisted of William Kennedy Smith, Timmy Shriver, Kara Kennedy, and Teddy Kennedy Jr.

■ When John was at Brown University, he kept a pig in the basement of his frat house with the intention of raising it and selling it for slaughter.

■ Also when John was at Brown, he pledged the Phi Psi fraternity and had to endure Hell Night, which involved swallowing goldfish; crawling around on a floor covered with animal entrails; grabbing a banana in a toilet bowl while blindfolded; and getting paddled.

■ John once showed up at a Halloween party in Manhattan dressed (although "undressed" would be a better word) as Michelangelo's *David*. He wore skimpy white tights, and his chest, face and hair were completely covered with talcum powder.

■ As an adult, John (and, presumably, Carolyn Bessette) sleeps in a queen-size brass bed.

■ John once chased after a guy to return a five-dollar bill that the man had dropped.

■ When John was fourteen and vacationing in Gstaad, he threw snowballs at the paparazzi who were following him and incessantly taking his picture.

Do you think John looks less than thrilled to be atop his steed Danny Boy? Probably so. John did not share his mother's and sister's passion for all things equestrian! This picture was taken in 1967 while the family was on vacation in Ireland. PHOTO: PHOTOFEST

■ When John stepped out of his limousine at the 1977 New York premiere of *Saturday Night Fever* the crowds in front of the theater lost all interest in the movie's star, John Travolta.

■ In 1987, when John couldn't get a first class plane ticket on a flight to West Palm Beach, he bought two coach seats: one for himself, and one for his guitar.

■ In the Eighties, John worked out at the Plus One Fitness Club in SoHo where a membership cost $6,000 a year. His fellow club members included Bernadette Peters and Cher.

■ When John was in his twenties, he used to occasionally help out at the 42nd Street Development Corporation, a real estate group that had been cofounded by his mother Jackie. He would take care of customers who would come in to pay their rent and one restauranteur remembered that John was always incredibly polite.

■ John owns a German Shepherd named Sam, and coowns with his wife, Carolyn Bessette, Friday, a white and black dog (seen in the "Brawl in the Park" videotape discussed in Chapter 6).

■ John's favorite vegetable is spinach. When he revealed this to Barbara Walters during her special, "The Ten Most Fascinating People of 1995," Walters replied, "Oh, you're going to be awfully popular with mothers all over America!"

John F. Kennedy Jr., Actor It probably started back when John was a toddler: Every Christmas, Caroline, John, and assorted Kennedy cousins would star in a production of a Nativity play for the gathered Kennedys. Later, however, Jackie was against John pursuing a career in acting. In March 1989, *Ladies Home Journal* reported that Jackie felt that acting was "undignified and potentially dangerous." In 1985, John costarred in the play *Winners* at the Irish Arts Center. He got rave reviews. Jackie (and John's sister Caroline) didn't attend,

Jackie and John leave Arlington National Cemetery after a 1969 visit to J.F.K.'s grave. John did not seem to mind leading the parade of assembled media and onlookers. PHOTO: PHOTOFEST

in protest against his appearing in the play. John allayed his mother's worries, however, when he told reporters that he was only doing the play for fun, not as a stepping-stone to an acting career.

Twelve J.F.K. Jr. Acting Roles

Oliver! John appeared as "Fagin" in this December 1971 Collegiate production. He was eleven, and this may have been his first "real" acting performance.

Petticoats and Union Suits John was fifteen and attending Phillips Academy when he appeared in this play in 1975. It was obvious that this was not just another student production when the play was reviewed by the *New York Times*. The *Times* theater critic wrote: "One can't help [but] be aware of the 15-year-old John Kennedy in his role, although like others in his celebrated family, he seems to be trying painfully to avoid special attention."

Comings and Goings John was seventeen in 1977 when he starred in this Phillips Academy production with then-girlfriend Jenny Christian.

A Comedy of Errors by William Shakespeare. John was eighteen when he appeared in this classic at Phillips in 1978.

One Flew Over the Cuckoo's Nest by Ken Kesey. John was nineteen when he starred in this play as "Randall P. McMurphy" (the role played by Jack Nicholson in the 1975 movie) in 1979. Jackie attended one of his performances and was reportedly quite upset by the scene in which John's character was suffocated. One of John's classmates said "[Jackie] had sort of a hard time with it. She was gasping."

Volpone by Ben Jonson. Opened March 14, 1980. John was twenty when he played "Bonario" in this Brown University production. His mother attended his first performance which was initially hailed by the *Brown Daily Herald*'s theater critic, but later the positive review was retracted. The critic said he was so overwhelmed by Jackie's presence (he sat next to her at the premiere) that he abandoned his critical judgment and gave John an unjustified glowing review.

The Tempest by William Shakespeare. John was twenty-one when he played as "Antonio" in this Shakespearean tragedy at Brown in May 1981. John was excited about doing Shakespeare (even though the critics were not too impressed with his performance) and he sent the notices to his uncle, actor Peter Lawford.

In the Boom Boom Room by David Rabe. John was twenty-two when he appeared in this Brown production in 1982. He played the boyfriend of a go-go dancer and got good reviews. One of the most remarked on elements of John's performance was the crew cut he wore for the role. John in short hair got as much attention as the female cast member who took her top off during the performance.

The Playboy of the Western World by J. M. Synge. John was twenty-two when he starred as "Christy Mahon" in this Brown production in 1982. Critics charged that he was miscast for the role, but his fellow actors almost unanimously praised his performance. John also had to come to terms with his celebrity and the fact that many people were going to attend the play simply because he was in it. He told the director that it was okay to mention that he was in the production, but that he did not want his appearance to be the focus of the advertising for the play.

Short Eyes by Miguel Piñero. John was twenty-three when he appeared as the child molester "Longshoe" in this 1983 school production, his last acting performance at Brown. He was very good in the role and one critic wrote that, "John played his part to perfection."

John (second from left) visited England around 1970 to spend the Christmas holidays with his aunt, Princess Lee Radziwill (far right). John's sister Caroline, standing behind Jackie, holds pine firs for holiday decorations. PHOTO: PHOTOFEST

Winners by Brian Friel. John costarred with then-girlfriend Christina Haag in August 1985 in this play produced by the Irish Arts Center in Manhattan. He was twenty-four at the time and played as an Irish teenager. The play ran for six performances and Jackie refused to attend any one of them, such was her displeasure with John's pursuit of acting roles. Sandy Boyer of the Irish Arts Center said of John's performance, "John is an extraordinary and very talented young actor who could have a very successful stage and film career if he wanted it."

A Matter of Degrees Made in 1988, released in 1990. This was a film directed by W. T. Morgan and produced by Randall Poster that starred Arye Gross (of the TV series *Ellen*) and Tom Sizemore (*Natural Born Killers*). John was twenty-eight when he made a cameo appearance as a "guitar-playing Romeo" in this drama about a college radio station. In the final cut of the film, John is shown singing exactly ten seconds of the Elvis Costello song, "Alison" (the producers could not get the rights for the song and so could not include John's entire performance in the movie).

■ When John was eighteen, producer Robert Stigwood offered him an opportunity to play his father as a young man in a movie about J.F.K.'s life. John was reportedly initially interested but turned Stigwood down when he learned how upset his mother was by the whole idea.

■ John likes to attend plays in Manhattan and often can be seen at Knicks basketball games.

■ John has often been seen on Monday nights in sports bars watching football games with his friends.

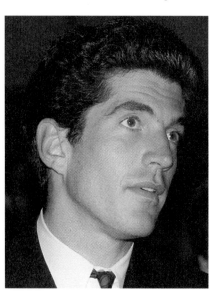

John has perfected ways of maintaining a calm demeanor when out in public, even when all eyes in the room are on him.
PHOTO: PHOTOFEST

■ John's reading tastes lean primarily toward non-fiction.

■ When John was thirteen, he was mugged in Central Park. He was riding an expensive ten-speed Italian bike when the mugger leaped from the bushes, reportedly shouted, "Get the hell off the bike!" and rode away. The thief was eventually caught, but Jackie refused to press charges because she knew it would turn into a media circus and she refused to subject John to that kind of publicity.

■ John always attaches his wallet to his pants with a chain. He has a fear of having his pocket picked.

■ Two of John's favorite alcoholic beverages are tequila and beer.

■ John learned to speak Greek in the years following his mother's marriage to Aristotle Onassis.

■ When a *National Enquirer* photographer tried to photograph John as he left Le Club after a birthday party for him and sister Caroline (they were eighteen and twenty-one, respectively), John's friends tried to stop the photographer and a fight broke out.

■ In 1991, John broke his leg playing football and ended up on crutches for a couple of months.

■ John can be a bit irresponsible. He continually forgets his keys when he leaves his apartment and, even with million dollar trust funds, he has been known to be in arrears on his rent.

■ In the spring of 1996, John received a notice from the State of New York that he was delinquent on his $300 attorney registration fee and that if he did not pay up within thirty days, he would be suspended and lose the right to practice law in New York. It is assumed he paid his fee.

■ John was once arrested in Connecticut for driving 81 miles per hour in a 55 mile per hour zone.

■ It seems as though John is a genuine and devoted exhibitionist. The book *Prince Charming* quoted TV personality Couri Hay, who worked out with John at the Aspen Club in Colorado, as saying, "He loves to walk around in the nude. . . . He walks around in the gym with his bathrobe open, and when he takes a shower he leaves the curtain open." From his behavior, Hay concluded that John "could have been a porno star." The book also recounted a story Hay told of a pool party at Hyannis Port during which John came out of the house wearing only a towel. When he took off the towel in front of everyone he was completely naked. He skinny-dipped in the pool for a while and then sauntered slowly out of the water, naked and wet, driving the gay waiters at the party absolutely crazy.

■ John writes left-handed and is a *terrible* speller. His handwritten invitations to his twenty-fifth birthday party at the Nirvana Club invited guests to come to the ". . . lessor of two evils."

One of the Good Guys   Here are some of the charitable organizations and causes John is involved with:

John leaving work at the D.A.'s office in New York in 1993. PHOTO: JOHN BARRETT, GLOBE PHOTOS INC.

His aunt Jean Kennedy Smith's Very Special Arts Program for people with learning and other disabilities

The *Profiles in Courage* Award

> In 1990, John and Caroline began presenting an award called the Profiles in Courage Award inspired by their father's intention in writing *Profiles in Courage*: "Without belittling the courage with which men have died, we should not forget those acts of courage with which men have lived." John also did an audio taping of his father's book and donated all the royalties to the Kennedy Library.

The Robin Hood Foundation (Board Member)

South African Group for Education (Founder)

The President's Committee on Mental Retardation

The Naked Angels Theater Troupe in NYC

Other members of this actors' group include Matthew Broderick, Rob Morrow, Marisa Tomei, and Fisher Stevens.

The Special Olympics

■ John once hung upside down and kissed the Blarney Stone during a visit to Ireland (an incident not out of the ordinary, as most visitors to the Emerald Isle can attest).

■ One of John's NYU Law School classmates told *People* magazine that often prospective employers would use up their entire twenty-minute interview with John satisfying their curiosity about him and his family instead of actually interviewing him for a position.

■ John's first paying job was at the New York City Office of Economic Development in 1986. John's mother was a member of the board of this organization.

■ On Tuesday, May 7, 1996, when John hopped on the Eighth Avenue subway to get home after a Rangers' game, he was recognized by his fellow passengers, but left alone. One New York newspaper wrote that this use of public transportation showed that even though John had made a fortune from the April 1996 auction of his mother's things, he still had "his feet on the ground."

John boating in the waters off stepfather Aristotle Onassis's Skorpios Island in 1970. The man with John is one of Onassis's bodyguards. The bodyguard ultimately chased away the photographer who took this picture.

PHOTO: PHOTOFEST

■ John researched his role as editor-in-chief of his own magazine *George* by attending a three-day seminar called "Starting Your Own Magazine."

■ At the press conference announcing *George*, John took a question from a Boston reporter. "I have to ask," the reporter began. "What's your home phone number?" The reporter, by the way, was male.

■ When John was a student at Collegiate, a teacher talking about the Sixties during class kept referring to "your father" instead of "President Kennedy." John's response? Total silence.

■ On the twentieth anniversary of the Brooklyn Restoration Project, John roller skated with a bunch of kids involved in the project. When a little kid asked him his name, John replied "John Kennedy," to which the boy excitedly replied, "He was one of our Presidents!" John smiled and said, "Yeah, I know. He was my dad."

■ According to Leo Damore, author of *Senatorial Privilege*, Jackie gave John an ultimatum when he told her he wanted to attend the Yale Drama School after graduating from Brown. She told him, "I'll disinherit you unless you go to law school." John went to law school.

Defensive Tactics When John is in public at a party or some other social gathering, he deftly uses almost imperceptible movements to turn his body so that his back faces people whom he senses are about to introduce themselves. He has perfected the use of body language so that he sends a silent yet unmistakable signal that he is not to be approached.

American royalty meets British royalty: John shakes hands with Queen Elizabeth II during the dedication of the Runnymede (England) memorial to J.F.K. Next to John is his mother Jackie, sister Caroline, uncle Robert Kennedy, uncle Ted Kennedy, and aunt Jean Kennedy Smith (William Kennedy Smith's mother). PHOTO: PHOTOFEST

Three "Titles" That Have Been Bestowed on John

1986: "One of America's Most Eligible Bachelors" (Manwatchers, a 10,000-member Los Angeles-based organization devoted to, well, watching men!)

June 16, 1986: "America's Most Eligible Bachelor" (*People*)

September 12, 1988: "Sexiest Man Alive" (*People*)

■ In early 1996, John stopped in at a small Manhattan restaurant, Ellen's Stardust Diner, for a quick breakfast before heading off to his job as editor of his new political magazine *George*. John was alone and while he ate, he read three New York newspapers. He finished his breakfast, paid the check, and left, leaving the three newspapers on the table. Even before the diner door slammed shut behind him, three young women leaped from their chairs and ran to where he had been sitting to retrieve these newfound collectibles: They each now owned a newspaper that had been touched and read by John F. Kennedy Jr.!

The Reluctant Politician John and Caroline campaigned during their Uncle Ted's bid to be the Democratic Presidential candidate in 1980. They stumped in out-of-the-way places in Vermont and Maine. John also introduced his uncle with his now-legendary speech at the 1988 Democratic convention. Talking about his uncle, John said:

He has shown an unwavering commitment for the poor, the elderly, for those without hope regardless of fashion or convention. He has shown that our hope is not lost idealism but a realistic possibility.

■ According to one of John's ex-girlfriends, John smokes exactly one cigarette a day, and he never succumbs to a craving for a second one.

■ In honor of his Irish heritage, John had a shamrock tattooed on his forearm in the summer of 1991.

■ In 1988, John's favorite restaurant was Jackson Hole on Columbus Avenue and Eighty-fifth Street in New York City. He has since been seen dining in a number of restaurants and clubs of all price ranges around Manhattan, including the "biker bar" Hogs & Heifers on Washington Street.

Notable Personal Traits Unceasing politeness and courteousness; impeccable manners; dignified bearing; playful demeanor.

■ When John cooks at home (which apparently isn't often) it's usually a pasta dish.

■ One of John's favorite movies is Woody Allen's *Broadway Danny Rose*.

■ When John was working in the Manhattan district attorney's office, he would often receive unsolicited photos of women in his mail. One woman once sent him a cappuccino machine.

■ John expects his employees to subscribe to his work ethic: Shortly after launching *George*, he issued a memo telling his staff that he expects to see all of them in the office when he arrives each morning at 9:30.

■ Someone attempted to blackmail John when he was in college. He told the story during an interview with former *National Enquirer* editor Iain Calder in the August 1996 issue of *George*:

> *When I was in college, I once got a call, and it was a British voice on the other end. He said, "We have information that you're gay, and we have photographs to prove it"—photographs taken in a bar or something. I said, no, it wasn't true. Then they called my uncle Teddy—who's used to getting odd bits of strange news about his nephews—and said: "We have these*

photographs of John, but if you pose for some Christmas pictures with your family, we may not run them."

John then asked Calder if that had been the *Enquirer* and Calder replied that is didn't sound like them because "it's so stupid to think a smart senator would fall for a transparently stupid line like like that."

■ John periodically visits his mother's acupuncturist for accupressure treatments for sore muscles and his back.

Sportin' Man   Some of John's favorite sports include **Bicycling** (In addition to distance riding, John often cycles around Manhattan, and was often seen mountain-biking to and from his office in New York when he was working for the District Attorney's office); **Camping**; **Diving**; **Fishing**; **Frisbee** (Often with a dog in a New York park); **Hiking**; **Kayaking** (John once wanted to buy a kayak company that made what he called the "Rolls Royce of kayaks," and distribute them nationally); **Rock climbing**; **Roller blading** (John has often been seen Roller blading around Manhattan and actually caused quite a stir when he and Daryl Hannah bladed to his mother's wake instead of arriving by car); **Roller skating** (John has attended and participated in roller skating parties to raise money for inner city charities and civic groups); **Rugby:** John played competitive rugby in college but left the team because he missed too many practices; **Skiing**; **Softball**; **Touch football** (A standard ritual at Kennedy family gatherings in Hyannis Port); **Whitewater rafting**; **Weight-lifting** (John worked out competitively with weights in college, "surprising those," according to *Growing Up Kennedy*, "who remembered that he was the least enthusiastic participant in many of the family [sporting] competitions"; and **Wrestling**.

Arnold Schwarzenegger and his wife, John's cousin Maria Shriver, arriving at the 1995 Special Olympics in New Haven, Connecticut.
PHOTO: ANNMARIE LEVATINO

The J.F.K. Jr. Travelog

Here is a look at a few of the many places John has visited (so far!) during his lifetime.

Africa   John spent several days lost in the forest of Mount Kenya in Africa during a seventy-day survival course in 1979.

The Aland Archipelago   The Aland Archipelago is a chain of islands in the southern stretch of the Gulf of Bothnia in the Baltic Sea between Finland and Sweden. John's trip to Ahvenanmaa (the main island) in the summer of 1992 afforded him the opportunity to become a professional travel writer. John and three friends kayaked throughout this island chain with John taking the role of navigator and cook. John's menus consisted mostly of spaghetti. John wrote an article for the *New York Times* travel section about the trip, for which he was paid $600. Here is an excerpt from his article:

> *The western winds rose and fell with the sun, and so we slept by day and paddled at night through still water, marveling at the extravagance of a sky where sunrise, sunset and moonrise occur almost simultaneously.*

The vistas in this region of the world are breathtaking beyond imagination and also quite dangerous for the inattentive. John wrote—in a matter-of-fact, self-effacing tone—of rescuing one of his friends who fell in the water and then carrying him to shore because his legs were numb from the cold.

Antigua   Jackie took John and Caroline to the Caribbean Island Antigua in 1965 when John was five. They stayed with millionaire Paul Mellon and his family.

Aspen, Colorado   John has visited Aspen several times for ski trips, including one with his mother and sister following Jackie's appearance at a United Nations Christmas concert in the late Sixties. Their first trip here seems to have been in 1965, when John was five. His uncle Bobby taught him how to ski.

The Berkshires, Massachusetts   When he was fifteen, John accompanied his uncle Ted and aunt Joan to the Berkshire Mountains for a skiing vacation.

The Caroline Islands   The Caroline Islands lie north of New Guinea in the Pacific, to the east of the Philippines. John and his cousin Timothy Shriver visited the islands in 1975 when John was fifteen and went scuba diving to explore sunken Japanese warships.

Cordoba, Argentina   In the late Sixties John spent some time here on the cattle ranch of Miguel Carcano, whose daughters were friends of John's uncles. While in Cordoba, John placed a stone on a monument that had been laid there by his father many years earlier.

France   John has visited France often, including trips with his mother in 1975, and a visit with then-girlfriend Carolyn Bessette in 1996.

Great Britain   Jackie and the children visited England for the dedication of the Kennedy Memorial at Runnymede in 1965. While there, John and Caroline's nanny, Maud Shaw took five-year-old John to the Tower of London. John spent his time in the Tower looking at the cannons and swords and asking countless questions about how executions and beheadings were carried out. He had absolutely no interest in seeing the Queen's Crown Jewels and instead wanted all the "gory details" about how they killed people in the Tower.

The group went to England with uncles Bobby and Teddy Kennedy, and Secretary of State Dean Rusk. Jackie and the children stayed in the home of his uncle, Prince Radziwill. They fed the ducks in Guen Park; saw the Changing of the Guard at Buckingham Palace; went to the Zoo in Regents Park; and Caroline went horseback riding in Rotten Row. Also, Caroline and John crawled into the barrel of a cannon while touring Buckingham Palace. Until John was four, the U. S. Marines and the American astronauts were his favorite heroes. After he saw the Changing of the Guard in London, Great Britain's distinguished Life Guards were briefly his favorites. While in London, John even interrogated a Beefeater guard about executions in Merry Olde England (we imagine he got no response).

At the Runnymede ceremony, the Queen dedicated a small plot of English soil to the memory of J.F.K. Nanny Shaw took Caroline and John to her family home in Sheerness for a weekend. John told Miss Shaw that he liked her house. He reportedly told her, "I like this dumpy little house," and was particularly pleased that the house only had one flight of stairs.

Greece   During his mother's years with Aristotle Onassis, John visited Onassis's island of Skorpios, as well as Athens and many other Greek sites.

Gstaad, Switzerland   Jackie took John and Caroline skiing in Gstaad in January 1966.

Hawaii   John's trip to Hawaii with his mother and uncle Peter Lawford's family in June 1966 unfortunately resulted in burn scars when John tripped and fell into a fire that had been put out but that was still smoldering. His Secret Service agent John Walsh grabbed him and rushed him to a doctor who diagnosed second degree burns on his right arm, right hand, and buttocks. He was treated and bandaged and was ultimately fine. If John still has scars today they do not show in photographs. (And I'm referring, of course, to his hand and arm. Photos of his butt have never appeared in print.)

India   John spent six months here in 1983 working with the poor; he also attended the University of Delhi where he studied food production and health care.

Ireland   John traveled to the Emerald Isle with his mother and Caroline in 1967 and while there, kissed the Blarney Stone and visited the Kennedy ancestral home in Duganstown. In one of those weird coincidences of history, the cab driver who drove John and his family around town was named John F. Kennedy.

Italy   One notable trip John made to Italy was in April 1996, during the Sotheby's auction of his mother's estate. John flew to Milan to meet with *George* advertisers and also to interview fashion designers Valentino and Versace. He also had lunch with designer Romeo Gigli and planned on interviewing some of Italy's newly-elected female politicians for the September issue of his magazine.

It was speculated that John intentionally scheduled this trip out of the country so that he would be unavailable during the Sotheby's auction but, of course, no one's talking. It does make sense, though, that John would want to remove himself from the absolutely insane media circus surrounding the auction.

Johannesburg, South Africa   John spent the summer of 1980 here working for a mining company owned by his mother's friend and companion Maurice Tempelsman.

Kenya, Africa   In the summer of 1979, John studied environmental issues on Mt. Kenya, just north of Nairobi in Kenya. This was one of John's many trips to Africa.

Maine   John spent twenty-six days in Maine as part of the Outward Bound survival course in June 1977 when he was sixteen. Part of the course required him to spend three days alone on an island with no food, two gallons of water, a small supply of matches, and a book on edible plants. The course toughened him up (which pleased his mother), although there was a Secret Service boat nearby just in case John got into serious trouble.

Mexico   John was six when he stayed with his mother in his aunt Lee Radziwill's Acapulco villa in March 1967 and is probably best remembered in Mexico for shooting a photographer in the face with a water pistol.

Rabinal, Guatemala   In the mid-Seventies, John spent a summer here, working with the Peace Corps helping victims of a devastating earthquake.

Russia   John visited Russia with his cousins Maria and Tim Shriver in 1975. Tim Shriver reported that John ate everything and that the rich food did not bother him at all. "[John] was a garbage can," Tim said.

St Barthélemy Island [St. Bart's], The Caribbean   This is where the nude photos of John were taken. (See "Scandals" for more details.)

St. Martin, The Caribbean   This is where John first met Daryl Hannah.

RISING SON: The Evolution of John

The world has watched John grow up. We saw him as a newborn in his mother's arms; we all watched as he matured and grew into a handsome and poised young man.

This photo feature takes a look at the evolution of John, beginning with Jackie holding him at age two, and concluding with a stunning shot of a "wet and wild" John as he appears today.

John at age 2 in Jackie's arms.
PHOTO: PHOTOFEST

John at age 6 during a visit to Hawaii.
PHOTO: PHOTOFEST

John at age 9 during a trip to Rockefeller Plaza with his mother to see the lighting of the huge 70-foot Christmas tree.
PHOTO: PHOTOFEST

John at age 10. He accompanied Jackie (second from left) and Caroline (second from right) to the Somerset Hills Pony Club for a horse show.
PHOTO: PHOTOFEST

John, age 13, and Jackie attended the 64th National Boat Show at the New York Coliseum in January of 1974. PHOTO: PHOTOFEST

Portrait of the Stud as a Young Man: John was around 17 in this picture and was rapidly developing his storied looks and physique. Okay, so he needed more time to work on his hair. PHOTO: BERT REAVLEY, PHOTOREPORTERS

John was a few months away from turning 16 when this picture of him and Jackie was snapped in the Montego Bay, Jamaica airport terminal (Is that Elvis to John's right!?) PHOTO: PHOTOFEST

John was days away from his 19th birthday when he attended the dedication of the John F. Kennedy Library in Boston. Caroline and Jackie stayed close by his side as he prepared to give his speech. PHOTO: PHOTOFEST

J.F.K. JR. REVEALED?

What Astrology, Numerology, and Graphology Have to Say About John Jr.

John Kennedy Jr. does not give interviews about himself. He speaks infrequently in public, usually at a press conference for his magazine or promoting some charitable endeavor in which he or his family are involved. He used to make campaign appearances for his relatives who were running for office but lately, since starting *George*, he hasn't been doing much of that either.

So how will we ever get to know this very private, reclusive scion of America's most famous family? Sadly, short of sitting in Starbucks and pounding down a dozen espressos with John as he bares his soul to us, we can't.

But we can have some fun with some amateur psychoanalysis of John by looking at his horoscope, the numerological makeup of his name, and his handwriting.

So, with tongue buried deeply in cheek, here is an "in-depth" look at America's favorite Kennedy.

The Planets, the Stars, and the Son: An Astrological Profile of John F. Kennedy Jr.

Astrology is the study of the positions of planets with an eye towards predicting their influence on human lives and events.

Astrology aficionados theorize that if the invisible pull of the moon can affect the tides *and* a woman's menstrual cycle, then isn't it possible that there are unseen, unidentified forces or vibrations emanating from the planets that can also impact humans in other ways?

Good question, and one that has been debated for millenia.

The author had an astrological profile done for John F. Kennedy Jr., using his birth date, time, and place (early morning, Friday, November 25, 1960, in Washington, D.C.). My astrologer, a terrific guy (who is also a massage therapist) named Paul Levatino, used a sophisticated computer program to generate John's chart and interpretations and, frankly, some of the results were amazing.

I will now go through some of the more intriguing comments from the profile and discuss them based on what we know to be facts about John Jr. (Interpretations that only John would be able to verify were omitted.)

Virgo Rising *"Others see you as a self-sufficient and rather self-contained person. You have a strong sense of propriety. Politeness, good manners, and correct behavior are important to you."*

John's bearing in public and irresolute politeness are legendary. Even the *paparazzi* say that his manners are impeccable. His mother taught him (and Caroline) well.

"You are not especially ambitious."

In the past, John has been criticized for appearing "rudderless" and content to coast through life. He is now perceived in the exact opposite way; as a focused and ambitious publisher and businessman.

Sun in Sagittarius *"You are . . . an adventurer at heart, one who loves to take risks, to discover and explore new worlds, and to take the untried path rather than the safe, reliable one. You need a lifestyle that provides opportunities for travel, movement, change, and meeting new people."*

This is right on the money. During his life, John has been on an Outward Bound survival endurance trip; worked in a South African diamond mine; helped rebuild homes in Guatemala after an earthquake; worked with the poor in India; and studied environmental issues in Kenya. He is an experienced world traveler and is willing to take risks.

"You probably traveled around and experimented with many different paths before you settled on a particular career."

John *has* traveled around and experimented with drama and the law before he settled (for now?) on a particular career (which, for now seems to be publishing).

"You have a sporting, playful attitude towards life and are philosophical about your mistakes. You have the ability to sense future trends, to see the big picture. . . . You do not take yourself too seriously.

John is a sports *animal.* He plays almost everything and has been photographed shirtless in Central Park so many times, people joke about whether he even owns a shirt. (He once broke a leg during a football game, ending up on crutches for weeks.) John's manner with the media (and also with people who approach him) is often playful and casual. When he failed the New York Bar Exam for the second time, he self-effacingly admitted that he was probably not "a legal genius." His driving philosophy for starting *George* was a belief that a new trend had emerged in which politics and popular culture were now merged in the social consciousness of the country and that the time was right to capitalize on this new and emerging climate.

"[Y]ou . . . do not do well with a possessive, clinging, or emotionally demanding partner."

Does the name Daryl Hannah ring a bell?

Mercury in Scorpio *"You . . . prefer learning through direct experience . . . rather than vicariously through books. You also have an instinctive rapport with animals, and you may feel you relate better to them than to people!"*

John has never been perceived as a great student. Even in grammar school, his mother wasn't happy with his grades. As for his rapport with animals, during the notorious "Brawl in the Park" with Carolyn Bessette, it was reported that John was yelling that she wasn't getting his dog if they broke up.

Mercury Sextile Venus *"You could develop great technical skill as a . . . creative writer. Your sense of humor, tact, and personal charm are a great benefit to you in any work with people on a one-to-one level."*

John's writing in *George* (assuming the stuff with his byline is actually written by him) is actually quite good, and his interviewing questions and editing are also above average. His father wrote; his sister writes; and his mother was a book editor; so maybe being the author of a prominent, nonfiction book or a novel might be in his future someday. As for his personal charm, talk is that the initial success of *George* was a result of John's personal charisma with advertisers and financial backers. As his partner Michael Berman expressed it, "Who's not going to return John Kennedy's call?"

Moon in Aquarius *"In your personal relationships, you insist upon a certain amount of independence and the freedom to pursue friendships with as many people, of both sexes, as you choose. You do not appreciate a jealous, possessive partner."*

Again, rumor has it that one of the reasons John and Daryl Hannah broke up was because she was too possessive. Also, there have been reports that Carolyn Bessette is quite jealous and that some of John's (supposedly innocent) dalliances with people like Sharon Stone and Cindy Crawford drove Carolyn crazy.

Venus in Capricorn *"You are old-fashioned about courtship and love, and will remain faithful to your loved one in good times and in bad."*

When Daryl Hannah had a fight with Jackson Browne that allegedly turned physical, John immediately got on a plane and flew to California to rescue her.

Venus Conjunct Jupiter *"You are bighearted and openhanded with both your money and your affections . . . pettiness or stinginess is foreign to your nature and you feel most comfortable in an elegant, beautiful atmosphere."*

John has a reputation for being a big tipper and has often been photographed kissing and hugging women in public. Also, he grew up surrounded by art, music, literature, antiques, and culture, and became accustomed to having servants take care of all of his needs. This backfired a bit on him when he first started living on his own. His apartment was reportedly a mess and he was very irresponsible about paying his rent and taking his keys. He had always been used to people doing things for him and he had to learn how to take care of himself.

"Gracious and charitable, you enjoy sponsoring social events or cultural activities."

This one's easy: Throughout his life John has appeared at fund-raisers and cultural events for a great many causes, ranging from the Special Olympics to literacy causes.

Venus Conjunct Saturn *"Perhaps due to painful relationships and separations in your early life, you do not trust others very easily, and it takes a long time to take down all of your barriers and defenses.*

I would call losing his father at the age of three a "painful separation in [his] early life," wouldn't you?

Venus Trine Pluto   *"You are charismatic and can have a powerful emotional influence on others, especially those of the opposite sex. You may use your attractiveness to manipulate others, sometimes without even realizing it."*

John F. Kennedy Jr.: Considered the "Sexiest Man Alive" in 1988. Case closed.

Venus Sextile Neptune   *"You are attracted to people with artistic . . . inclination."*

In the past few years, John has been linked with over a dozen models and actresses, including Sarah Jessica Parker, Sharon Stone, Ashley Richardson, Madonna, Cindy Crawford, Daryl Hannah, Melanie Griffith, Julia Roberts, and Elle MacPherson.

By the Numbers:
A Numerological Reading of John F. Kennedy Jr.

Numerology is an intriguing form of divination in which numbers are said to possess prognosticative powers and be capable of revealing insightful information about the person being "read."

Numerology aficionados (whose hero is the Greek philosopher and mathematician Pythagoras) cite as intuitive evidence of the magical power of numbers the pervasive belief held by many people that certain numbers are lucky or unlucky.

According to numerologists, leaning *toward* certain "lucky" numbers, such as 3, 7, or 9; and *away* from certain "unlucky" numbers, such as 13 and 666 is a subconscious acknowledgment of numbers' sway over our life paths.

Here, then, is a brief numerological reading of John F. Kennedy Jr., based on his birth date and name.

John was born on November 25, 1960. For our first reading, we add together the digits of his birth date, 11/25/1960:

$$1 + 1 + 2 + 5 + 1 + 9 + 6 + 0 = 25$$

We then add these two digits to arrive at his one-digit birth force number:

$$2 + 5 = 7$$

John Kennedy's birth force number, then, is 25/7.

Birth Force Number 7   The key word here is STUDY. The number 7 person is very cerebral, both intellectually and intuitively. He is very interested in introspection, meditation, and the search for perfection. This is the soul who needs to get away from society, to get back to nature, to think in the forest or on a mountaintop. Number 7s need to specialize in something in order to succeed financially. They need to know everything there is to know about a subject, and they will drive themselves unmercifully to attain that goal and be "the best." At his worst, the number 7 can be secretive, gossipy, overly analytical, or cynical. Their desire to be the best can get the best of them, causing low energy and sometimes even illness, the function of which is to slow them down so that they can listen to their wisdom. This is the person who thinks he can accomplish superhuman tasks in a single day. Seven is the number of safety and of occult intelligence in the Kabbalah. The person whose number is 7 *must* regularly get "in touch" with his needs and listen to the innner self.

We should also look at the components of the birth forces number 7, the 2 and the 5, in order to determine where the 7 came from.

The 2 reveals that John will be the "reasoning force in any situation," and that he is capable of seeing both sides of an argument. The 2 also paints him as "group-oriented" and hints that "he might display some amount of acting ability." At his worst, he can be shy, self-conscious, and reclusive.

The 5 in John's birth force number reveals that he is "an independent traveler who loves his freedom" and that he "will likely . . . be sexually attractive." The 5 tells us that John is a good decision maker and at his worst, might be overly self-indulgent and, at times, "no fun at all to be around." (See what model Janice Dickinson had to say about her date with John in the chapter "Isn't It Romantic?")

To complete this brief numerological reading we will now look at his "soul number," his "personality number," and his "integrated self number," all of which are determined by examining his name. We need to assign a numerical value to each letter in his name using the following chart:

1	2	3	4	5	6	7	8	9
A	B	C	D	E	F	G	H	I
J	K	L	M	N	O	P	Q	R
S	T	U	V	W	X	Y	Z	

John Fitzgerald Kennedy Jr. thus, is "scored" as follows:

VOWELS:	6	9	5 1	5	5 7
	J O H N	F I T Z G E R A L D	K E N N E D Y	J R
CONSONANTS:	1 8 5 6	2 8 7 9 3 4	2 5 5 4	1 9

John's *soul number* (which is supposed to reveal what a person is *inside*) is calculated by adding together the values of all the *vowels* in his name:

$$6 + 9 + 5 + 1 + 5 + 5 + 7 = 38$$
$$3 + 8 = 11$$
$$1 + 1 = 2$$

John's soul number, then, is **38/2**. Interestingly, this reading gives us another 2, which is explained above in the discussion of John's birth force number.

Next, we calculate John's *personality number* by adding together the values of all the *consonants* in his name. (This number is supposed to reveal the way a person appears to others):

$$1 + 8 + 5 + 6 + 2 + 8 + 7 + 9 + 3 + 4 + 2 + 5 + 5 + 4 + 1 + 9 = 79$$
$$7 + 9 = 16$$
$$1 + 6 = 7$$

Again, another 7 appears, which is the defining number of John's birth force number.

The final step in John's numerological reading is to calculate his *integrated self number*. This number is calculated by adding together the single-digit soul and personality numbers:

$$2 \text{ (soul)} + 7 \text{ (personality)} = 9$$

John's integrated self number of 9 reveals that he is motivated by idealism and that he is concerned with humanitarian causes. Again, dramatic ability is indicated, as is the tendency to possibly change direction when he is on the verge of success. Interestingly, one of the characteristics of a 9 is that he may love himself a little too much.

Numerology can be looked upon as a fun tool for self-analysis. Even if you believe that this intricate calculating of numerical values has no real meaning, any assessment of a person's personality can stimulate a self-evaluation, thus possibly leading to insight and motivation for change. For instance, if a numerological reading indicates that a person is narrow-minded and self-absorbed, this kind of in-your-face confrontation may help a person see and correct certain personality flaws.

In John's case, based on our knowledge of his activities and interests since his childhood, there is a great deal in his reading that hits the mark, wouldn't you say?

In His Own Hand: A Handwriting Analysis of John F. Kennedy Jr.

Our handwriting can reveal quite a bit about us. Graphologist Nadya Olyanova, author of four books on graphology, says, "Handwriting is really mindwriting. It's a photograph of how your mind works."

Graphology is used today in business, law enforcement, and even medicine as a tool to help reveal personality traits, motivations, and the inner workings of a subject's mind.

A true graphology reading usually requires a page or two of a person's handwriting. We do not have a page or two of John's handwriting, but we do have his signature: It is reproduced at the bottom of his "Editor's Letter" in every issue of his magazine *George*. Also, in the December 1995/January 1996 issue, John wrote the words "Happy Holidays" above his signature, which was slightly different than the signature used in the other issues. These extra bits of writing were helpful for this profile.

This "reading" does not pretend to be comprehensive, but rather a fun look at what John's handwriting might indicate about his personality, based on eleven basic elements of handwriting analysis: slant, baseline, margins, spacing, pressure, size, connectedness, lead-in strokes, endings, capitals, and individual letter analysis.

Slant   The slant of a person's writing is measured on a scale ranging from an extreme leftward slant to an extreme forward slant. Introversion is indicated by a slant to the left; extroversion, by a slant to the right. The severity of the slant indicates the degree of extroversion or introversion. This scale is known as the graphology "Emotional Barometer" and is the first element looked at.

John's writing has a modest forward (extroversion) slant. According to Gittelson, this ". . . . indicates a healthy attitude toward the future, without ignoring the lessons of the past, as well as a good balance of emotion with pragmatism."

Baseline   The baseline is a measure of how much a person's writing slants uphill, downhill, or if it lies perfectly straight across.

John's writing climbs slightly uphill. This indicates "an optimistic attitude towards life and a character whose actions are often shaped by enthusiasm."

Margins   Margins are used to evaluate a person's attitude towards money as well as how generous he or she is. Since John's writing appears at the bottom of a page and there's no way of knowing what size margins he uses, we'll have to skip this one.

Spacing   The spacing between words is supposed to indicate a person's generosity as well as his feelings and attitudes about his own "personal space." There are three degrees of spacing: lots of space between words; a moderate amount, and tightly packed.

John's writing seems to fall into the second category, indicating someone who is outgoing and gregarious and who enjoys the company of other people. It also hints at someone who is not adverse to sharing his ideas and emotions with others.

Pressure   To accurately gauge the pressure of a writing sample, it is necessary to feel the back of the page. Since that's impossible, we'll pass this one, too.

Size of Letters   Graphologists look to the size of a person's letters as an indication of the "volume" with which a person metaphorically speaks through his handwriting. There are four categories of size: small, medium, large and extra large.

John's writing seems to fall between the medium and large category. The medium component of his letters indicates a fairly normal person, while the large quality, according to Gittelson, hints at an individual who "likes to do things right, and usually that means big." He also reveals that such a person "likes himself and you might, too."

Connectedness The connectedness of a person's writing is an indicator of how the person thinks. There are three grades of connectedness: completely connected; somewhat connected with some breaks; and almost completely disconnected.

John's writing falls into the second category. This says that he manifests a nice balance of logical thinking combined with flashes of intuition, which he can recognize and knows how to use. It also shows that he has strong powers of concentration and reasoning.

Lead–In Strokes and Endings Lead–ins are those slopes that begin letters and which can be eliminated without losing the recognizability of the letter. The endings of letters are looked at for their upward or downward slope.

John uses lead–ins for most of his words and letters, indicating a relatively normal and balanced personality. It also hints at someone who is a firm believer in tradition and decorum. This is not surprising when we consider Jackie's contribution to his adult personality.

John's endings usually slope up, indicating "An affable person who likes to be surrounded by others. Not a loner in any way. This person is probably very likable and socially stimulating."

Capitals John's capitals are a mixture of script and block letters. This could suggest an occasional lack of consistency in certain situations.

Individual Letters Often, the way a person crosses his t's, dots his i's, and draws his looped letters can reveal a great deal about their personality.

In John's case, he dotted his "i" in "Holidays" up and to the right of the letter. This is supposed to indicate enthusiasm.

Interestingly, there are three "y" letters in "Happy Holidays—John Kennedy" and John wrote each one differently. Also, the "p" letters in "Happy" and the "J" in "John" are also looped letters.

The "y" loop in "Happy" is normal, which indicates someone who is realistic; the "y" loop in "Holidays" is angular, which indicates aggressiveness; and the "y" loop in "Kennedy" is swooping, which indicates a preoccupation with the physical.

John's "p" loops are both normal.

As for the ascending loops for the letters "l"; "d"; and "h"; they are all of a style known as compressed, meaning they look like a straight line. This is supposed to indicate repression of some sort.

John Kennedy Jr.'s handwriting bears out much of what we know about him, and it also illuminates certain aspects of his personality that we have seen realized in his career choices, hobbies, and personal bearing.

ISN'T IT ROMANTIC? A BEVY OF THE WOMEN IN (OR RUMORED TO BE IN) J.F.K. JR.'S LIFE

As the former most eligible bachelor in the United States (perhaps in the world), John F. Kennedy Jr. could literally date (and bed?) almost anyone he wanted.

As we've already seen, although he is not a rock star, an actor, a bestselling novelist, or a politician (yet?), John Kennedy has groupies. Every eye in the room lands on him when he makes an entrance and women of all ages swoon at the sight of him.

He is a deft social mingler and has elevated small talk to an art form. He has a presence that comes off as warm and friendly, but he is actually rather guarded in public situations.

This chapter looks at almost three dozen women who have been linked with John by countless newspaper and magazine articles, Kennedy biographies, and tabloid TV shows. (The ladies' names are in alphabetical order.)

Disclaimer: Let's face it: Only John and the women on this list know the actual truth of their rumored relationships. All we're doing here is looking at some of what the media have written about John and his love life over the past decade or so.

The singer Appolonia, one of the women John has reportedly dated.
PHOTO: PHOTOFEST

Appolonia   Appolonia is best known for once being the main squeeze of the artist who used to be called Prince but who lately has been known as The Artist Formerly Known as Prince Who Signs His Name With Some Kind of Strange Hieroglyphic-Looking Symbol. She costarred with Prince in the film, *Purple Rain* (1984).

It isn't known how many times John and Appolonia dated, but it was apparently just one more of John's many relationships that didn't really go anywhere.

Do you think John got to meet Prince, though? And if Appolonia did introduce him, what do you think John called him?

Audra Avizienis   In 1988, stunning model Audra Avizienis had this to say about her relationship with John: "We've been on a few dates, but I'm not seeing him."

John with future wife Carolyn Bessette at the Municipal Arts Society at the Lexington Avenue Armory in February of 1996. PHOTO: ROBERT SPENCER, RETNA

At the time, Audra was twenty–two and John was twenty–seven. Audra was with Click, the modeling agency that also represented supermodels Veronica Webb and Elle MacPherson, as well as Raquel Welch's daughter Tahnee; Liv Ullman's daughter Linn; Tommy Chong's daughter Robbie; Peter Lawford's son Chris; and Gregory Peck's daughter Cecilia. (Perhaps John's family connection to Chris Lawford resulted in an introduction to Audra? Just wondering.)

"I'm not a girlfriend," Audra told *People* magazine. "He has a girlfriend. Or have they broken up?" She then went on to describe John further: "He has this quiet sadness. There's something pensive and sad about him."

Meg Azozi   John was photographed out on a date with Meg Azozi in 1977 when he was seventeen. Their picture reappeared years later in the August 16, 1993 issue of *People* magazine.

John wore a rumpled sport coat and pants and a white shirt open at the collar and had a lit cigarette in his left hand. He was still a bit ungainly and had not yet evolved the looks and manner for which he is so well known today, a personal style many have described as that of a male model.

Meg had a naked "deer in the headlights" expression on her face, her eyes wide with apprehension at what may have been her first exposure to the incredible media attention John gets whenever he goes out in public. Even at seventeen, though, John was a seasoned pro when it came to being in the spotlight and the *paparazzi* attention did not seem to bother him in the least.

John and Meg dated at least through the summer of 1977, when John worked as an usher at the Robert F. Kennedy Tennis Tournament in Forest Hills. Meg had a front row seat at the event and John sat next to her when he had a break in his ushering duties.

Julie Baker   Julie Baker is a Wilhelmina model who is one of a looooong line of gorgeous models that John has dated.

Julie looks exactly like John's mother Jackie and the two of them dated for a time after the Daryl Hannah years. Julie's roommate Christy Orr was a witness to John and Julie's relationship and spoke to John Jr. biographer Wendy Leigh about their time together. Christy told her, "They didn't go out too much but spent most of the time in our apartment in the Village, watching TV or just talking. He took her to some avant-garde shows downtown and he was sweet and romantic and brought her flowers. He was also nice to me. I was going on a trip to Latin America, and he told me what vitamins I should take while I was down there."

Reportedly, John and Julie were extremely close during the time they dated and were actually seen at one point petting and French kissing at a party.

Paula Barbieri   When the videotape of John and Carolyn Bessette's 1996 argument in a New York park aired on CBS-TV's *Day & Date*, someone on the show speculated that the reason for the fight was because John had gotten involved with O.J. Simpson's ex-girlfriend, model, and actress Paula Barbieri, and Carolyn had found out about their affair. Paula's people deny that Paula and John had anything to do with each other and there has been no official comment from John or his people regarding this rumor.

Only in the United States could such disparate elements as interracial sex, the modeling business, "America's Royal Family," "America's Fallen Football Idol," and the "Crime of the Century," come together so smoothly and synthesize into unrelenting gossip.

Carolyn Bessette

> The family welcomes Carolyn with open arms.
> **—MARIA SHRIVER**

> Carolyn has her own sense of mystery, doesn't she?
> **—LETITIA BALDRIDGE**

Carolyn Bessette, a six-foot tall, blue-eyed beauty with a brain, has been John's wife—Carolyn Bessette Kennedy—since Saturday, September 21, 1996. She had been his live-in girlfriend since the spring of 1995.

Carolyn was born in 1967 in White Plains, New York and grew up in tony Greenwich, Connecticut. Her mother, Ann Marie, is a public school administrator, her father, William, now divorced from her mother, sells cabinets in New Rochelle, New York. Carolyn's stepfather, Richard Freemen, is an orthopedist.

Carolyn was voted "The Ultimate Beautiful Person" by her classmates at St. Mary's High School and reportedly was a favorite even with her friends' *parents*. She graduated from St. Mary's in 1983 and then went on to Boston University, where she graduated in 1988 with a Bachelor's degree in elementary education. While in college, she modeled for a calendar titled *B.U.'s Most Beautiful Women*. In 1990, Carolyn also modeled for fashion photographer Bobby DiMarzo, a Boston shutterbug who was quick to sell rights to his pictures of Carolyn immediately after news of the wedding hit the press. The October 8, 1996 issue of the *Globe* ran seven pictures of Carolyn from this session, including two incredibly sexy (and possibly embarrassing to John?) shots. One showed her sitting in a haystack with her legs spread and her dress pulled up high enough to expose her bare thighs. Another was a very erotic still of her wearing a deeply plunging blouse, open enough to show cleavage.

In early 1996, The *New York Post* quoted a photographer who once shot pictures of Carolyn as saying, "She was the most beautiful girl I ever photographed. She could have modeled full-time, but she wasn't interested. She couldn't sit still long enough. I think she's so smart, she wanted a better job."

Carolyn once dated John Cullen, now an acclaimed hockey player with the Tampa Bay Lightning, and Calvin Klein model Michael Bergin. She also was romantically linked with Alessandro Benetton, the heir to the Benetton fashion fortune.

He's got the look! Here a young John shows the sex appeal that has made him a consummate ladies' man and world class "date" (until he settled down with Carolyn Bessette, that is!).
PHOTO: BERT REAVLEY, PHOTO REPORTERS

After her graduation from Boston University, Carolyn took a Boston-based marketing job with the Lyons Group, handling bookings for two nightclubs. (She was described by someone who worked with her as "a good schmoozer.") The *New York Post* quoted a friend of Carolyn's: "She hated it. So when she got offered a job at Calvin Klein, she jumped."

She worked for a time at the Calvin Klein store in Chestnut Hill in Massachusetts and then was transferred to the New York offices where she worked as a Public Relations executive and where—so the story goes—she ultimately met John.

Legend has it that John met her when he visited Calvin Klein and she was assigned to him as his personal shopper. (The other version of their meeting has them connecting during a stroll in Central Park.) A confidential source who knows Carolyn very well and who often double-dated with her told the author that she would guess that the notorious blow-up in a New York park in early 1996 was probably Carolyn's fault. A source told the author that she had witnessed Carolyn's temper firsthand. She also said that Carolyn could be very domineering when she wanted to be.

John gave Carolyn an emerald and diamond ring which insiders called a "friendship" ring because if anyone who knew either of them admitted it was an engagement ring (which it was), the media attention would be merciless. (This is the ring that was damaged when John ripped it off Carolyn's finger during their fight in New York but it has since been repaired.)

In April 1996, John and Carolyn traveled to France and their visit was covered in a two-page spread in the *National Enquirer* titled, "Springtime in Paris with JFK Jr. and his ladylove."

John and Carolyn walked along the Right Bank and visited the Museum of Modern Art and were seen hugging and kissing. The article speculated that because Carolyn always kept her coat buttoned over her belly when they were out in public she might be pregnant, once again fueling a rumor that many who know the couple have denied.

It seemed almost inevitable that John would marry Carolyn. They were together a long time, and the fact that they argued publicly was nothing more than a sign that they have a healthy, normal relationship. Carolyn has the intelligence, breeding, and style worthy of the Kennedy name and she will no doubt be able to handle the fame that comes with being Carolyn Bessette Kennedy.

Naomi Campbell

Even though John has been linked with a number of supermodels, in the case of Naomi Campbell, the connection seems to have been decidedly one–way.

According to an article in the June 1996 issue of *Cosmopolitan* magazine, Naomi once tried to have John "summoned" to her as she dined in a trendy New York restaurant.

The story goes that Naomi was at Cafe Tabac when she noticed John sitting at another table. Naomi called over her waitress and instructed her to go retrieve John and bring him to her table. The waitress complied but when she told John of Naomi's request, he simply shook his head no and went back to his dinner.

Supermodels are, if anything, used to being catered to in ways most of us cannot even begin to imagine. But John F. Kennedy Jr. is not your normal testosterone-driven slobbering babe-hound leering on the sidelines waiting for a chance to just make eye contact with one of these magazine mannequins. John may, in fact, very well *be* a slobbering babe–hound, but he has the good taste and enviable discretion not to parade his lusts in public. One does not summon John F. Kennedy Jr., especially a model whose entire claim to fame relies on her looks.

Nonetheless, Naomi was (still is?) narcissistic enough to demand John's presence at her table. When she was informed that John refused to come over, she became so enraged that she stalked out of Cafe Tabac, leaving her five hundred dollar tab unpaid. And, of course, her hapless waitress was left tipless.

Jenny Christian

Jenny Christian was John's girlfriend during his time at Phillips Academy in Andover, Massachusetts and for a short time after that.

John first met Jenny when he was sixteen, a few months after he arrived at Phillips. She was a gorgeous blonde and one of the most sought after girls on campus, and John fell for her almost immediately.

In a recent lengthy interview, one of Jenny's quotes sticks out (and illustrates the kind of girl she was and explains why John was attracted to her): "If he had fallen out of a pickup truck he still would have been irresistible to me. He was extremely handsome, nice, and sweet. It was a great romance."

Jenny apparently didn't care that John was a Kennedy and that he was a celebrity in his own right. She liked John for John and he must have found this intoxicating. All his life, he has been President Kennedy's son first and "just John" second. People's perceptions of him were always inspired by his image, and until John met Jenny, most girls who wanted to date him simply wanted to move in the circle of his celebrity.

Jenny, on the other hand, was apparently easy-going and self-assured. Like John, she had a privileged upbringing. Her father was a surgeon and she attended one of the most prestigious Ivy League prep schools, a place where she would get the best education possible and also meet people like John F. Kennedy Jr.

In 1977, John and Jenny starred in a production of the play *Comings and Goings* at Andover. They were very good together and their widely-known real-life relationship gave their performances an added dash of excitement and charm.

John and Jenny continued dating through his years at Andover and Jenny was warmly welcomed into the Kennedy clique. She was poised and pleasant and came from a nice society family and Jackie took to her immediately. This acceptance extended to being automatically included in Kennedy family functions. Jenny also accompanied John and the family on vacation trips during their time together.

In a truly ironic twist in the John F. Kennedy Jr. story, Jenny Christian was involved with John when he first met the woman with whom he would have his most public and talked-about relationship, Daryl Hannah.

In 1978, when John and Jenny were both eighteen, John was still at Phillips and Jenny had gone on to Harvard where she was majoring in psychology. The two were still involved, however, and Jenny accompanied John (along with his mother and the Radziwills) to St. Martin for a vacation. They all stayed at the beautiful La Samanna resort where, coincidentally, Daryl Hannah was also staying. Daryl was also eighteen at the time and was not yet as famous as she would be a few short years later. She had appeared in Brian DePalma's *The Fury*, but she was still six years away from the movie that would make her a star, Ron Howard's *Splash*. (*Hard Country*, *Summer Lovers*, and *Blade Runner* would come first.)

At this point in her life, however, Daryl was, according to an eyewitness, "really strange," and apparently carried a teddy bear with her whenever she was out in public. John and Jenny had the opportunity to meet her but it doesn't seem like there were any sparks flying between John and Daryl. In fact, Leigh's source reported that "John and Jenny seemed to think [Daryl] was weird and laughed a bit about her, but not in a malicious way." Daryl had a chubby face and was apparently extremely shy and so it's understandable that John would not be attracted to her then, especially considering the fact that he had the sophisticated and beautiful Jenny Christian with him at the time. (This was around the time that Daryl's yearbook reported that she had "nob knees" and a "potty mouth." Even odder is the quotation Daryl used for her yearbook picture: She quoted six lines from a Jackson Browne song that went "Pretty little one/How's it all begun?/They're teaching you/how to walk—/But you're already on/the run.")

Ten years later, John and Daryl would meet again. This time, however, both of them were quite a bit different both in maturity and personal situations. Daryl had starred in *Splash, Reckless, Roxanne, Wall Street, Legal Eagles,* and *The Clan of the Cave Bear* by now and was a major star, and they would end up a couple.

After St. Martin's, though, John and Jenny Christian remained a twosome and Jenny accompanied his family to John's Phillips Academy graduation ceremony.

As is often the case, though, distance was a relationship killer for John and Jenny. Jenny continued her studies at Harvard while John remained in New York. By 1980, they had split up for good but remained friends. John is known for ending romances on good terms and remaining close with his ex-girlfriends. Jenny Christian reportedly still has warm feelings for John and recently spoke highly of him.

Cindy Crawford

John and model extraordinaire Cindy first met in 1987 when John was in college and Cindy commanded that he somehow be persuaded to attend her twenty-first birthday party. John, who was twenty-six at the time, showed up and they reportedly dated a few times but then nothing more seemed to come of their relationship.

Later, there were published rumors that John had a fling with Cindy when they were working together as she posed for the cover of the first issue of *George*. A source close to John's para-

Supermodel Cindy Crawford, displaying the form that John Jr. obviously admires. He did, after all, put her on the cover of the first issue of *George*! PHOTO: PHOTOFEST

mour Carolyn Bessette is reported as telling the *National Enquirer* that John denies that anything happened between him and Cindy, and that even though they went out for dinner a few times, it was strictly business. This makes sense: Many sources have confirmed that John seems to remain good friends with many of his ex-girlfriends and the fact that the biggest supermodel in the world happily posed for the first issue of his new magazine would seem to indicate that Cindy and John maintained a closeness over the past decade or so.

If the two of them ever did get together, can you imagine what their kid might look like?

Diana, Princess of Wales

People magazine once reported the following: "Princess Diana was reportedly crestfallen when Kennedy was a no-show at a Manhattan luncheon she attended last winter."

There have been countless newspaper stories and gossip column items about Diana's alleged determination to meet and have a relationship with John.

The tabloids have repeatedly run stories quoting unnamed "royal insiders" who claim that Diana is feuding with her sister-in-law Sarah Ferguson over who will win John's heart.

Kitty Kelley has said "I know for a fact that Princess Diana would very much like to meet J.F.K. Jr. When you think about it, it's a beautiful coupling."

Janice Dickinson

John has dated *a lot*, no doubt about it, and model Janice Dickinson is one of those many names he has been linked with in the newspaper gossip columns and in magazine profiles.

Of course, John never talks about the women in his life and if Dickinson has ever discussed her reported date (or dates?) with John, it has not been in a forum that has been widely disseminated. Their alleged romance may have been a brief fling that only the two of them know the duration of, or perhaps the press reports could have been nothing more than a reporter seeing them together for whatever reason (business, friendship, etc.) and planting an item that linked them romantically. As of now, nobody's talking so we can only speculate.

Someone who *has* talked, however, is Michael Gross, the author of *Model: The Ugly Business of Beautiful Women*.

In his book, Gross reveals some titillating details about Janice Dickinson and, since these stories are apparently true, John probably had his hands full with her. She is sultry, dark, and small breasted, with a look that was extremely well-received in Paris in 1975. She was ambitious and determined to make it in modeling and she was frank and blunt about it: "My purpose was to work as a model, become a star, and go back and make the big bucks." She willingly agreed to nude photos and some of her nudes are extremely dramatic and erotic.

She became one of the biggest modeling stars in the eighties. Christie Brinkley was the blond model in demand; Janice Dickinson was the dark–haired beauty everyone wanted. She developed a reputation for outrageous behavior, taking off her clothes and dancing in a fountain in Italy, and reportedly doing prodigious quantities of drugs. She got involved with Sylvester Stallone and claimed that he was the father of her first child. He admitted paternity but then DNA tests proved he *wasn't* the father.

Janice Dickinson is now just over forty and works as a professional photographer. She was only briefly linked with John and it is likely that she—like that other wild woman John dated, Madonna—was somewhat out of John's league both sexually and in her experience with recreational drug use.

But since he is John F. Kennedy Jr., if he wanted to date a supermodel, he dated a supermodel. And, thus, one more name has been added to this list.

Sarah Ferguson, Duchess of York

As far back as the spring of 1995, there was talk that Sarah Ferguson (known affectionately around the world as "Fergie") was extremely interested in meeting and possibly dating John F. Kennedy Jr.

Fergie, who was married to England's Prince Andrew before their divorce in 1996, is reportedly a sex, money, and fame junkie. Tabloids around the world have published photos of her in extremely bawdy (and embarrassing to the British monarchy) situations. Fergie has been photographed topless on a beach and, in what was her most notoriously infamous series of photos, seen getting her toes sucked erotically on a beach by American businessman Johnny Bryan. (Apparently John would have to cultivate a foot fetish to satisfy the Duchess if they ever did get together, eh?)

London newspapers originally ran stories alleging that Fergie was so hung up on John that she went on a makeover program involving losing weight, a change of hairstyles, and new clothes, so that when she finally did get to meet him, he'd be so overwhelmed by her charm and beauty, he'd fall for her in a flash.

One tabloid (quoting, of course, the ubiquitous unnamed "royal insider") reported that a psychic had told Sarah that she and John would ultimately end up together and Fergie then began referring to John as "Ken." Friends told the British papers that Fergie said, "Everything will be OK when I marry Ken."

So far, John and Fergie have not even met, let alone had a relationship of any kind. As America's former most eligible bachelor, John has often been linked romantically with women in the tabloids, but this Fergie situation is mega-weird: If the rumors are true, Fergie is determined to snare John, no matter what.

Who knows if she'll be deterred by the fact that he is now married to Carolyn Bessette?

In October of 1996, a British psychic named Madame Vasso Kortesis went public with the fact that she had been advising Fergie for years and that she had been tape-recording the Duchess's most intimate revelations. One was that Fergie had told her that she fantasized about marrying John and becoming his First Lady in the White House. Another was that Fergie "rated" her men from 1 (worst) to 10 (best) and that Texas oilman Steve Wyatt was number 1; Prince Andrew was number 2; toe-sucking Johnny Bryan was number 3; and—get this—John F. Kennedy Jr.—whom she has never even met—was ranked number 9.

Christina Goodman

Christina was John's very first girlfriend. He met her at the Chase Golf and Tennis Camp in Bethlehem, New Hampshire when he was fifteen. Christina attended the Spence School in New York and dated John for about a year after their time spent together at the camp.

Melanie Griffith

Actress Melanie Griffith, who was once reportedly seen out on the town with John. She was probably wearing more than this at the time, though. PHOTO: PHOTOFEST

Again, this is one of those cases where someone reported seeing John out with actress Melanie Griffith (who has been involved with, alternately, Don Johnson and Antonio Banderas for years) and it was, of course, interpreted as a date.

It could have been business, or Melanie and John could be friends. No one except the two of them really knows, and, so far, no one's talking.

Christina Haag

Christina Haag is a gorgeous brunette who looks like a youthful combination of actresses Dana Delaney and Andie MacDowell. She is the daughter of a marketing executive, and a graduate of the Brearley School in Manhattan. She has known John since they were both fifteen. They were fellow students at Brown University.

She once worked as a hat–check girl in an Italian restaurant and as an assistant to a fashion designer.

Christina and John acted together (as lovers) in Brian Friel's play *Winners*, and she and John rented a house together in the summer of 1988 in Venice, California when she appeared in *Sleeping With the Past* at the Tiffany Theater in Hollywood.

John was quite enamored of Christina but was not above fooling around with other women behind her back when he was dating her. He dated Daryl Hannah in October 1988 when he was still seeing Christina and Daryl was still involved with Jackson Browne.

Jackie liked Christina a lot and when Christina's father died in 1992, Jackie Onassis visited Christina at her apartment to express her sympathy, even though John and Christina had broken up years earlier. It has also been reported that Jackie was not above lending Christina one of her own designer gowns when she had to go out on the town with John.

In May 1989, John took Christina to see *Miami Blues* (the Alec Baldwin thriller) with his cousin, William Kennedy Smith, but was not very attentive to her throughout the night.

It is also reported that John once took Christina to the Russian Tea Room, but shortly after they arrived, he suddenly came down with a headache and took her home. He quickly returned to the restaurant, however, with a blonde on his arm.

In addition to appearing together in *Winners*, John and Christina also appeared together in the 1991 film *A Matter of Degrees* in which John had a ten second cameo. John played the guitar and sang the Elvis Costello song, "Alison." He and Christina both attended the premiere of the film at the Bleecker Street Cinema in New York on September 13, 1991. Their relationship was essentially over by then, however, and Haag told a John Jr. biographer that their split was "amicable." In 1996, Christina starred in the horror movie *The Mantis Murder*, and has also appeared in many television productions.

Interesting Footnote: Actress Molly Ringwald, who reportedly also dated John, attended the premiere of Christina Haag's new movie *The Mantis Murder*. Wonder if they had anything to say to each other? Maybe they compared notes?

**Daryl Hannah,
one of John's
most visible and
high-profile
relationships.
They split for good
in August 1994.**
PHOTO: AUTHOR'S
COLLECTION

Daryl Hannah

Daryl Hannah's relationship with John Kennedy was the one that received the most attention throughout the world.

During their time together, there were countless newspaper articles and TV segments about the pairing of John and the sexy blond *Splash* star, as well as the August 16, 1993 issue of *People* magazine that had a cover story that shouted, "IT'S LOVE!"

This union had it all: America's most eligible bachelor was dating a gorgeous blond movie star (who also happened to be wealthy in her own right). Hollywood had met Camelot, and the speculation about whether or not these two would eventually marry drove Kennedy watchers crazy.

John and Daryl first met in 1978 when they were both eighteen and vacationing with their families on the Caribbean island of St. Martin. They met again years later at the September 1988 wedding of John's aunt Lee Radziwill to *Steel Magnolias* director Herb Ross. (Daryl had starred in the film with Shirley MacLaine, Dolly Parton, and Sally Field. The film was released in 1989.)

John and Daryl's 1988 wedding meeting was due to the intercession of Daryl's wealthy and powerful stepfather Jerry Wexler. Daryl had expressed an interest in meeting John and Wexler used his friendship with John's uncle Ted

Kennedy to get Daryl invited to the Radziwill-Ross wedding (which didn't seem at all inappropriate since Daryl had recently worked on *Steel Magnolias*).

John and Daryl hit it off immediately and after the wedding, they began dating, even though John was still dating others, including actress Sarah Jessica Parker. Daryl was also still involved with singer Jackson Browne, with whom she shared a $2.5 million home in California.

Daryl and John's first official date was in early October of that year and the media covered it as though it was a summit meeting of the utmost importance. John probably should have been honest with Christina Haag and ended their relationship when he started dating Daryl, but he didn't. Instead, he manipulated the situation so that Daryl was his private, sexy secret.

John had several not–so–secret rendezvous with Daryl (the tabloids were watching the two of them like hawks) throughout 1989 and it seemed as though it was only a matter of time before John broke up with Christina and went public with his relationship with Daryl.

In the summer of 1989, however, Daryl and Jackson Browne got back together after a very rocky period and Daryl told John she couldn't see him anymore. (Some John watchers assert that one of the reasons he failed the New York Bar exam the first time he tried it was that he took the test shortly after Daryl moved back in with Browne.) John and Daryl's separation would last for almost three years until just before the September 1992 incident at Daryl and Jackson Browne's California house during which Daryl was apparently assaulted. John and Daryl kept in touch during this period of separation but Daryl was adamant that she wanted her relationship with Browne to work. Daryl and John occasionally saw each other during this time and once, when Daryl got sick in Brazil while filming *At Play in the Fields of the Lord*, John had a thousand roses sent to her hospital room.

In late September 1992, on a visit to Manhattan, Daryl decided that she wanted to be with John and she immediately flew back to California to break up with Jackson and get her things. A fight broke out between the two of them and the police were called. This is where the stories differ. Friends of Daryl's have said that Jackson got violent when she told him she was leaving him. Daryl did not press charges against Jackson Browne, and the singer said the following about allegations that he beat her:

> It was untrue that I was violent, and it was untrue that the argument was about possessions and things she was trying to remove. Daryl's father [Jerry Wexler] was dying. She was under tremendous pressure and had been caring for him over a month in the hospital. So she was in very fragile shape. We had been breaking up for quite a while. Absolutely no assault occurred.

Jerry Wexler's brother Haskell told a dramatically different story however:

Jackson beat Daryl in September 1992. I was with her in the hospital. I saw ugly black bruises on her eye and chin and on her ribs. The examining doctor reported she had blood in her urine. The doctor was shocked by the severity and noted Daryl as "a badly battered woman." I photographed her in the hospital.

Daryl's own mother Sue Wexler said the following in the August 16, 1993 issue of *People* magazine:

I saw her shortly after in the hospital. I saw the damage that was done to her. The doctor was very concerned. Jackson was a very, very good friend of mine, but when I saw Daryl, I just felt betrayed.

When John heard about what had happened he immediately flew to California. After a couple of days on the West Coast, they both flew back to New York where John nursed her back to health.

This incident cemented their hibernating relationship and for the following year they were a definite couple. The two were seen together all over Manhattan and Daryl even accompanied John to his ten year reunion at Brown University. John later visited Daryl on the Los Angeles set of her HBO movie, *Attack of the 50-Foot Woman*. The happy couple moved in together, traveled together (the Philippines, the South Pacific, Switzerland, Hong Kong, and Vietnam) and Daryl supported John through the diagnosis of his mother's lymphoma. She later attended Jackie's funeral at his side.

Throughout this period, the media seemed to watch every move they made and speculations that the two were planning on marrying were as frequent and common as pictures of John with his shirt off. Daryl's purchase of an antique wedding gown at a flea market made national news, and even John's sister Caroline had to repeatedly deny that the two were getting married.

Ultimately, it was much ado about nothing and in August 1994, John and Daryl split up after a relationship that had had repeated ups and downs and starts and stops over a six-year period.

Rumor has it that Daryl wanted to marry John so badly that it scared the hell out of him and sent him into the arms of Carolyn Bessette. Novelist Sugar Rautbord, a friend of Daryl's, once said, "Daryl really liked him. She was *desperate* to marry him."

In January 1995, a close friend of Daryl's told *Good Housekeeping* magazine that Daryl was actually doing better without John: "For the first time in her life, she's not up to her neck with some guy."

Toni Kotite

John was linked with this theatrical director in 1993, during a period when he was reportedly seen out with a number of models and actresses. The press

likes to interpret John's dating habits as proof of the old adage, "Like father, like son;" but even though John loves women and dated a lot before he apparently settled down with Carolyn Bessette, it appears that he is what *Cosmopolitan* magazine described as a "serial monogamist": He does date a lot, but he's faithful to his girlfriend when he's in a relationship.

Elle MacPherson

Late in 1995, the British newspaper *The Sunday Mirror* ran a story that claimed that John had left steamy voicemail phone messages for supermodel Elle MacPherson when she was staying at the Beverly Hills Hotel.

Elle MacPherson at the Special Olympics. In late 1995, a British tabloid linked John and Elle, but both issued strong denials that there was anything going on between them. PHOTO: ANNMARIE LEVATINO

It reported that a former receptionist at the hotel was trying to sell the tapes for $50,000. The recordings allegedly have John telling Elle, "I wanna do it with you," "You are the fantasy I long to fulfill," "You have such nice buns," and "What I fantasize doing to you I can only reveal when we are alone together."

The *National Enquirer* picked up the story from the British paper and ran it in their January 2, 1996 issue. In the *Enquirer* piece, a ubiquitous "close friend" of John's is quoted as saying, "John is so offended and angry that he's telling friends, 'When I find the people responsible for this I'm going to strangle them with my bare hands.'"

Elle MacPherson's manager denied that Elle and John were even friends and the *Enquirer* quotes another source as saying, "John has no interest in Elle. He's devoting eighteen hours a day, seven days a week to his magazine, and his free time he spends with Carolyn. John told me, 'These rumors coming out of England infuriate me!'"

John's personal assistant RoseMarie Terenzio told the *Enquirer*, "There is absolutely no truth to this story. Mr. Kennedy has not called Elle MacPherson and left any messages."

Madonna

Many Madonna watchers believe that John F. Kennedy Jr. was pursued by the outspoken and sexually aggressive Italian American chanteuse as the final step in her inheritance (some say calculated hijacking) of America's Marilyn Monroe mythology.

In the early years of her career, Madonna devoted herself to a reinvention of her image in the mold of Marilyn. Her intentions were at their most blatant when she made her "Material Girl" video in which she recreated with meticulous attention to detail Marilyn's legendary red-gowned, song and dance routine from the 1953 film, *Gentlemen Prefer Blondes*, in which Marilyn performed the song, "Diamonds Are a Girl's Best Friend."

Madonna biographer Christopher Andersen wrote, "As undisputed heiress to the Monroe persona, she confided to friends that she felt fated to consummate a relationship with Kennedy's only son."

Whether or not this is completely true (or Madonna's *sole* motivation for seeking out John) is really known only by Madonna.

Granted, Madonna Louise Ciccone *is* an incredibly shrewd professional when it comes to her career, and yet it is hard to imagine even her being so chillingly crass as to set out to sexually seduce someone *only* as a career move. The father of Madonna's child is, after all, a mere fitness trainer; not exactly a union that elevates her social or professional standing. (Although it should be noted that she *has* been known to use dating as a publicity tool—her Grammy "date" with Michael Jackson a case in point, for example).

The Marilyn Factor probably intrigued Madonna and gave her a sense of history (as well as assuring herself of a place in the grand scheme of things) but one cannot help but speculate that her pursuit of John was more lust motivated, than history inspired.

Madonna is a sexual dynamo and John oozes sex appeal from every pore. Some have claimed that Madonna wanted John just so that she could add him to her long list of sexual conquests. That is probably an overly simplistic reading of a complex woman's motives. Let's put it this way: If John F. Kennedy Jr. was (heaven forfend!) short, fat, balding, and had a skin problem, a hunchback, and a limp, do you think Madonna would have pursued him sexually simply because he was the son of Marilyn Monroe's paramour? Not bloody likely!

Madonna began her *Quest for John* by acquiring his private home phone number and leaving him many messages on his answering machine. "Let's get together," she repeatedly suggested, until John finally took the bait.

Their first date was classic Madonna: She invited him to one of her concerts at Madison Square Garden.

There could not have been a more intimidating venue for a first date. At all of her concerts, Madonna is God. Not only did John get to witness thousands and thousands of people absolutely manic with adoration for her, he also got to see what it was like backstage at one of these events. The backstage scene after a Madonna concert is essentially a Madonna lovefest, overflowing with sycophants, celebrities, hangers-on, staff, security, and groupies; all there to try and snag even a moment with their idol.

According to reports, on this night Madonna deliberately ignored John (as well as TV star Don Johnson), and left him to cool his heels in a corner as she bestowed her attention on several of her favorites of the moment, one of whom was an obscure black graffiti artist known as Futura 2000.

John, who had grown up knowing how to remain dignified and unflustered in tense social situations, kept his cool, even though he was a bit bewildered by this turn of events. Why was this woman who had seemed so enthusiastic about meeting him suddenly ignoring him and treating him like a nobody? It was all part of Madonna's social and sexual gamesmanship and John just happened to be her latest victim. Eventually Madonna did turn her attention to John and their date progressed from there on along more traditional lines.

Apparently, John was not insulted by Madonna's childish treatment of him and so they mutually agreed to go out on an actual dinner date. During this time they were also meeting at the health club where they both worked out and going to great lengths to keep their relationship secret. One person, however, who was quite aware of John and Madonna's budding romance was John's mother Jackie. And to say that Jackie was less than thrilled with the idea of her son dating Madonna is an understatement of gigantic proportions.

On the evening of John's first official date out at a restaurant with Madonna, Jackie got wind of the get together and left numerous messages for John wanting to know what was going on. John thought this was amusing and seemed not to realize how his mother was perceiving—and reacting to—his romance with Madonna.

Her only son—the light of her life—was dating a sexually-charged woman who was deliberately modeling herself after the woman with whom his father had had one of his most torrid affairs. Jackie saw this as much more than just a casual fling. She was terrified that Madonna would possess her son the way Marilyn had possessed her husband. Madonna, on the other hand, found Jackie's curiosity about her hilarious. She even crowed to her friend Erika Belle, "Can you imagine how far I've gone? Jackie O wants to know all about me!"

John is, if anything, a devoted son, and so, to allay his mother's fears and show his respect, he invited Madonna to Jackie's apartment so the two could meet in private.

Madonna signed the Guest Register "Mrs. Sean Penn" and was probably on her best behavior. Reports of the meeting indicate that Jackie was as courteous and gracious as ever, but extremely guarded, if not actually cold, to Madonna. Christopher Andersen wrote that John said his mother "hit the roof" after Madonna left and read him the riot act.

Jackie warned him that Madonna was only out for herself and that she was using him and his name for publicity. Another friend of John's told Andersen, "It must have been like Marilyn coming back from the grave, this time to steal her son instead of her husband. It was a nightmare for her."

Jackie was also livid about a couple of other elements to this relationship: First, that John was dating a married woman and second, that Madonna used religious items in her act, something Jackie felt was sacrilegious. But a friend of John's told Andersen that the only thing Jackie was not the least bit concerned about was that Madonna was after John for his money. Even conservatively, he guessed, Madonna was at least ten times richer than John—and Jackie knew it.

Even though his mother was upset with him for seeing Madonna, John continued to date her, the two of them being extremely careful to keep their romance a secret.

As their flirtation progressed, it eventually became physical, and many of Madonna's and John's friends feel that their sexual incompatibility was probably what split them up.

As anyone who has seen Madonna's photo book, *Sex*, can attest, the Material Girl is a sexual virtuoso. If sex were a high school, she'd be in the advanced class. She apparently is familiar with S and M, lesbianism, interracial sex, and multiple partners; and she is also an uninhibited exhibitionist who reportedly prefers sex partners as wild and experienced as herself.

From all reports, John did not measure up to Madonna's usual standards. A friend of Madonna's has revealed that Madonna described John as an "innocent" and said that he was too shy and reserved for her tastes.

After a short romance that had the tabloids frothing at the mouth and wild-eyed with every salacious detail (real or imagined) they were able to conjure up, Madonna and John split up, but still remained friends. It seems as though they became like brother and sister after their unsuccessful attempts at a more intimate bond. Madonna reportedly called John in Los Angeles when he was interning at a law firm for advice about her deteriorating marriage to Sean Penn and, most tellingly, Madonna happily contributed an essay—"If I Were President"—as well as a sexy photo of her in a blue bikini straddling a diving board, to the first issue of John's magazine, *George*.

John and Madonna are apparently still good friends although neither, of course, will talk on the record about the other.

Regardless of the truth, however, theirs was the kind of short-lived tryst that made worldwide headlines because of the level of fame and celebrity attached individually to each of them. Combined, John and Madonna were a Force of Fame greater than either one of them on their own.

Sally Munro

There's an old adage that asserts that we all have a twin somewhere in the world.

Sally Munro, who was one year ahead of John at Brown University and whom he dated on and off for about five years, probably has already met her twin: Sally is a Caroline Kennedy look–alike. And I don't mean that Sally and Caroline have a faint resemblance in build, or hair color, or eyes. What I'm saying is that if you put a picture of each woman side by side, it would be difficult to discern who was who; that's how close this resemblance actually is.

John dated Sally through 1984, but they split up shortly thereafter. One thing we do know about John and Sally's relationship is that they would occasionally watch X–rated movies together. Wendy Leigh relates a story told to her by a video store clerk in which John and Sally asked to see the adult films list in his store. John asked Sally to pick one out. She closed her eyes and pointed to the list. Her finger landed on *Bodacious*, and that was the one they rented.

Singer Sinead O'Connor, a woman who dissed John and who saves a lot of money on shampoo.
PHOTO: PHOTOFEST

Sinead O'Connor

Irish singer and songwriter Sinead O'Connor hates the Catholic Church and the Pope with such a vengeance that during a 1992 appearance on *Saturday Night Live*, she tore up a picture of Pope John Paul II at the end of her musical performance. No one on the show knew that the shaved-head beauty was going to do it and the audience, instead of applauding at the conclusion of her a capella song, just sat there in stunned silence as the director quickly went to a commercial.

Now, if there was ever a family in America known for and associated with their religion, it would have to be the Kennedys and Catholicism. The fervent devotion to the Church by every single Kennedy makes John's hapless attempt at a relationship with Sinead O'Connor a social blunder of epic proportions.

In the summer of 1990, John and Daryl Hannah were at one of those incredibly trendy parties in Manhattan that most of us will never have the opportunity to attend. Sinead O'Connor was also at the party and John supposedly eyed her for quite a while before seizing on the right time to make his move. Daryl had been with John most of the evening but then she left him briefly to go to the bathroom.

John waited until she was out of sight, took a pen out of his pocket, walked up to Sinead, and introduced himself.

He then proffered his pen and asked her for her phone number.

Sinead leveled those gorgeous eyes of hers on John, and reached for his pen. But instead of writing down her number and handing it back to him, Sinead broke his pen in half and jammed the two pieces into John's shirt pocket.

John walked away and spent the rest of the evening with Daryl Hannah. Two years later, on October 3, 1992, Sinead shredded the Pope.

Boy, she sure hates Catholics, doesn't she?

Catherine Oxenberg

New York–born actress Catherine Oxenberg was hot for a time in the eighties when she played Amanda Carrington on the incredibly successful ABC series *Dynasty.*

Reportedly John and Catherine dated briefly, but nothing came of it. Catherine did some film work after her stint on the prime time soap, most notably playing Princess Diana in 1993's trashy *Charles and Diana: A Palace Divided.* In yet another example of just how weird things can sometimes get when you talk about the rich and the famous and what goes on in their lives, John Jr. would later be linked with the *real* Princess Diana, who reportedly has been pursuing a relationship with America's very own Prince. But in the eighties, John dated an ersatz Diana instead of the real thing.

Actress Catherine Oxenberg, who briefly dated John when she was a hot star in the Eighties. PHOTO: PHOTOFEST

Actress Sarah Jessica Parker on the beach. Was she waiting for John? PHOTO: PHOTOFEST

Sarah Jessica Parker

This fetching actress has been living with actor Matthew Broderick for years now, but she did date John briefly in 1991. She had been living with Robert Downey Jr. when she met John and they dated through the summer of 1991. She and John were sighted making out on a beach in the Hamptons, but when she flew to Las Vegas to film *Honeymoon in Vegas*, the romance was over.

Sarah has told reporters, "It's unfair, as a woman, to have to stand next to [John.]"

Ashley Richardson

Yet one more gorgeous six-foot, blonde supermodel John dated.

Actress Molly Ringwald, who recently returned to the United States after a self-imposed exile in Paris. Maybe she finally got over her breakup with John?
PHOTO: PHOTOFEST

Molly Ringwald

John dated redheaded actress Molly Ringwald briefly, but their romantic relationship was supposedly replaced by a strong friendship.

Julia Roberts

It is the nature of John's celebrity that any contact he may have with a woman is reported as something of significance when, in many cases, it is nothing more than an innocent lunch or business meeting.

This seems to be the case with Julia Roberts, one of Hollywood's highest-paid female movie stars.

The story goes that John was seen in May 1990 having lunch with Julia Roberts by the side of the pool at the swanky Four Seasons Hotel. He and Julia were allegedly seen by one of the hotel's security guards, who, to this day, is confident that they did, indeed, dine together.

John, as usual, has never commented on his lunch date nor denied or confirmed that he even met with Julia Roberts while in California. Julia, on the other hand, was queried by the press shortly after the security guard told what he had seen, and she denied not only having lunch with John but also said that she had never even met him.

Well, it seems as though John and Julia Roberts have now at least *met* since their alleged lunch: The Pretty Woman was one of the elite guests at the party John's sister Caroline gave on October 10, 1996 to celebrate her brother's marriage to Carolyn Bessette.

Stephanie Schmid

Not much is known about this tall lanky blonde who, it seems, has never spoken out about her time with John.

What *is* known is that sources close to Schmid have gone on record as confirming that John had a two-day affair with Stephanie during the period in the spring of 1990 when he was in California supposedly preparing for his third try at the New York bar exam.

Actress Julia Roberts claimed she never even met John, even though they were reportedly seen together in California. Now it's known that they are, indeed, friends.
PHOTO: PHOTOFEST

Stephanie, who was born in Texas and was twenty-two when she met John on Venice Beach, was given the complete J.F.K. Jr. treatment during their two-day romantic fling. They were seen dining at the Four Seasons (the same hotel where John was also supposedly seen with Julia Roberts during this time) and one of Stephanie's friends said that John treated Stephanie like a queen—and then apparently moved on.

Claudia Schiffer

Jeannette Walls of *Esquire* magazine alleged that John and Claudia Schiffer were involved at one point and that their relationship might have had something to do with the big fight John had with live-in lover Carolyn Bessette in a New York park in early 1996.

Gorgeous supermodel Claudia Schiffer has been engaged to magician David Copperfield for quite a while now so Walls may be totally off base. And yet Walls *did* say it on TV and usually, television gossip columnists can provide sources (usually anonymous) for their tips.

There has not been any official statements from either Schiffer or John's camp, and shortly after John and Carolyn's fight in the park, the reconciled couple attended a black tie function and seemed to be in fine fettle.

Can we even begin to imagine what the children of two people who look like John and Claudia would look like? When you look up physical attractiveness in the dictionary, you see pictures of these two.

Could John and Claudia have had a fling?

John has always been attracted to women who look like Claudia. Isn't it possible that he saw the clandestine nude photos of Claudia that appeared in *Penthouse* magazine and, much the way Madonna pursued him, he decided he had to meet this vision of erotic beauty?

Sure it's possible, but neither of them has spoken out about this, so any speculation is just that. It's an interesting coupling, though, isn't it?

Sharon Stone, another gorgeous actress John has been linked with in the press.
PHOTO: AUTHOR'S COLLECTION

Princess Stephanie of Monaco

Yet another rich and famous beauty John has allegedly been linked with.

Sharon Stone

Rumor has it that John and megastar Sharon Stone had a brief fling in the summer of 1995. Art Buchwald wrote a humorous column about their alleged romance and yet Sharon Stone, in a lengthy interview in the November 1995 issue of *GQ*, does not mention John even once.

Actress Brooke Shields, one of John's longtime friends and the star of her own sitcom, *Suddenly Susan*.
PHOTO: PHOTOFEST

Brooke Shields

John first met Brooke when she was sixteen and modeling for Calvin Klein. Brooke and her mother came to tour Brown University when John was attending there, and he actually acted as their tour guide. They had lunch together but never hit it off romantically.

Xuxa

Since 1994, Xuxa (whose real name is Maria da Garca Meneghel) has hosted a kid's TV show in her native Brazil called *Xuxa!* Twelve years prior to that gig, however, Xuxa appeared in a racy Brazilian flick called *Love Strange Love* in which she appeared topless in several scenes.

Xuxa met John Kennedy Jr. in early 1992 after she had her manager send his office a videotape and photograph with the message that she would like to meet him. (It has never been revealed what was on the video Xuxa sent John, but since she had a choice between sending clips from her children's show or clips from *Love Strange Love*, and since she *was* boldly seeking a date with John, it is not farfetched to imagine that she sent him a video of her at her sexiest, right?)

Xuxa is quoted as saying that she was first attracted to John after she saw his picture in a magazine (if anything, John may be one of the most photogenic guys on the planet) and thus, decided to pursue a meeting.

John took the bait and agreed to meet Xuxa for a lunch at Robert De Niro's TriBeCa Grill. Xuxa went straight to the restaurant and her manager, Rose Ganguzza, went to the District Attorney's office to pick up John in a limo. John refused to be seen getting into a limousine in front of the office where he worked, so the two of them walked to the restaurant where Xuxa was waiting for them.

Wendy Leigh reports that their lunch was repeatedly interrupted by people seeking autographs from Xuxa, and yet no one approached John for *his* signature. John and Xuxa got along quite well and after their lunch, John and Xuxa walked through TriBeCa, and then went their separate ways.

They didn't date again and John continued to see others in an attempt to soothe his grief over his breakup with Daryl Hannah.

But then something happened that made John realize that he had been shrewdly conned into being seen in public with billionaire Xuxa, a woman who apparently knew how to work the media on her own behalf. On Valentine's Day 1992, the tabloid TV show *A Current Affair* broadcast video footage of John and Xuxa's *entire date*. Xuxa denied to Wendy Leigh that she had deliberately planned the secret guerrilla surveillance of the date, but she did acknowledge that "Lots of people work for me, and I didn't know that one of them contacted the television show. I think that kind of publicity is bad for me."

Right. Being seen in public in the United States on a date with John F. Kennedy Jr. is bad publicity for an unknown (in the U.S.) South American TV star eager to break into the American market. Sure it is.

It is quite possible that the entire encounter was staged in a duplicitous way of getting Xuxa media attention in America. After all, does it make any sense at all that an obscure Brazilian children's TV show hostess would be blitzed by autograph seekers at a trendy New York restaurant and yet John F. Kennedy Jr.—who lives in TriBeCa and is easily recognized—would be ignored?

Regardless of the truth, to this day John believes he was set up and Xuxa continues to deny that she knew anything about it.

Xuxa has still not managed to establish a foothold on American TV. Serves her right.

JACKIE AND CAROLINE

There has always just been the three of us, my mother, Caroline, and me.

—JOHN F. KENNEDY JR., from *Growing Up Kennedy*

I understand the pressure you'll forever have to endure as a Kennedy, even though we brought you into this world as an innocent. You, especially, have a place in history.

No matter what course in life you choose, all I can ask is that you and Caroline continue to make me, the Kennedy family, and yourself proud.

—One of Jackie's final notes to John, written shortly before her death.

Jackie

President Kennedy's assassination created a bond between mother and son that was probably greater than it would have been had John Kennedy lived to see his son grow to adulthood. Jackie felt a powerful and compelling impulse to protect her children. John (and, of course, Caroline) felt likewise about shielding their mother from assassination junkies, the media, and just plain kooks, as well as sparing her—as much as possible—unnecessarily painful memories and experiences.

From all accounts, Jackie began worrying about John's well-being from the day of her husband's funeral. Throughout his childhood, both in Washington and later in New York, she made sure that there were always men in John's life

Jackie tried very hard to give her two beloved children as normal a life as possible. Here she keeps Caroline close by her side and a firm grip on John's hand as they all leave the Runnymede dedication in England. PHOTO: PHOTOFEST

Jackie two years after John was born. Her beauty and grace captured the world's attention. PHOTO: PHOTOFEST

to serve as positive role models and to act as surrogate father figures as he was growing up.

John's beloved uncle Bobby (Robert F. Kennedy) played this role until *he* was brutally assassinated. Secret Service agents, friends of the family, and, later, Aristotle Onassis, all played a part in shepherding John through childhood, adolescence, and into adulthood.

Jackie once remarked to a friend that she was afraid John would grow up to be "a fruit" if he did not have enough male companionship. She saw to it that he most assuredly did have such companionship and she also deliberately filled his summer vacations with extremely "masculine" activities, including wilderness training, camping, and other endeavors specifically designed to toughen John up and make him as self-reliant as possible.

Jackie's strategy worked.

John, as an adult, is truly a "man's man." He is athletic, has a great many male friends, loves women, and is poised and self-confident.

And until her death, John was always extremely solicitous of his mother; watching over her with a tender attentiveness that bespoke genuine affection, heartfelt respect, and great pride.

Jackie worried about John. She monitored the women he dated, and made it clear to him when she felt he was dating someone she felt was somewhat, shall we say, "inappropriate" for him. Jackie also guided John in his career choices, steering him away from the banal and prosaic (at least for someone with John's esteemed family name and history) career of acting, and into the higher calling of law, the profession his sister Caroline had chosen, and the one that would serve him well if he ever did decide to enter the "family business" of politics.

John's uncle, Senator Edward "Teddy" Kennedy, expressed the depth and beauty of John and Caroline's relationship with their mother in his eulogy for Jackie:

> *[Jackie's] love for Caroline and John was deep and unqualified. She reveled in their accomplishments, she hurt with their sorrows, and she felt sheer joy and delight in spending time with them. At the mere mention of their names, Jackie's eyes would shine and her smile would grow bigger.*
>
> *She once said that if you "bungle raising your children, nothing else much matters in life." She didn't bungle. Once again, she showed how to do the most important thing of all, and do it right. . . .*

Jackie was adamant about maintaining her privacy and she enlisted her children in this pursuit by giving them strict orders not to talk to the media unless the situation warranted it and the interview was rigidly controlled.

For the most part, Caroline and John bowed to her wishes, refusing any and all interview requests.

John has perfected the smooth, yet meaningless response, elevating it to a celebrity art form. When dodging the press is *completely* impossible, John will answer what are usually pointed and prying questions with flip, jocular responses that amount to a great deal of nothing. He is the consummate diplomat when dealing with the press and as a result, the reporters who cover him on a regular basis will usually cut him some slack and leave him alone when he asks them to.

When Jackie got sick, John was more attentive to her than ever before. He called her constantly, visited her often, and reportedly took an apartment near hers just so he could be close by in case she needed him.

When Jackie died, John lost the person who was probably the most special friend he will ever have in his life.

From the January 1995 issue of *Good Housekeeping* magazine:

John comported himself faultlessly during Jackie's final illness. After she died, he paid her the highest filial respect, in private as well as in public. He was proud of his mother's talents, her vivid intellect, her gift for words, her elegance that was a habit of mind as well as of appearance. When he came down from her apartment to announce her death—a simple, good-hearted, generously worded statement—to waiting reporters, he accepted the moment and rose to the gravitas of the occasion. At the funeral, after President Clinton bade Jackie farewell at the Arlington grave site, John wiped a tear from his eye. He thus gave the appropriate salute once again.

JOHN'S ANNOUNCEMENT TO THE MEDIA OF HIS MOTHER'S DEATH ON FRIDAY, MAY 20, 1994

Last night, at around ten fifteen, my mother passed on. She was surrounded by her friends and her family and her books and the people and things she loved.

And she did it her own way and on her own terms, and we all feel lucky for that and now she's in God's hands.

There has been an enormous outpouring of good wishes from everyone, both in New York and beyond. And I speak for all of my family when we say we're extremely grateful. Everyone's been very generous. And I hope now that, you know, we can just have these next couple of days in relative peace.

John with mom Jackie and her late-in-life companion Maurice Tempelsman. Shortly before she died, she wrote to John, "Stay loyal to those who love you. Especially Maurice. He's a decent man with an abundance of common sense. You would do well to seek his advice."
PHOTO: PHOTOFEST

Caroline

I'm not like everyone else. I'm Caroline Kennedy.

—CAROLINE KENNEDY, during her teenage years.

John and Caroline each had one of the most unique childhoods in American history. Of course they were born to wealth and social standing, but the assassination of their father when they were both young defined them in a whole new way and must be viewed as the seminal event in their lives.

Caroline is now a lawyer and a writer, although she, like her brother, does not practice law anymore. She is married to Edwin Schlossberg, fourteen years her senior, a smart and erudite businessman who has been an important influence on Caroline's financial well-being and intellectual growth.

Caroline has written two books with her co-author, Ellen Alderman: *In Our Defense: The Bill of Rights in Action*, which was a best-seller; and 1995's well-received *The Right to Privacy*.

As children, John and Caroline were typical siblings; alternately loving and affectionate and then, bickering and competitive. Many of the Kennedy biographies provide entertaining and revealing anecdotes about John and Caroline's childhood years together and can be found in most bookstores. (*Growing Up Kennedy*; *White House Nannie*; *The Kennedys: An American Drama*; *A Woman Named Jackie*; and *A Day in the Life of President Kennedy* are especially recommended.)

John and Caroline at ages thirteen and fifteen respectively, both wearing far more hair than they should have! The two were listening to their uncle Ted talk about the early seventies gasoline shortage. PHOTO: PHOTOFEST

Today, Caroline and John are best friends. John was Caroline's husband Ed's best man at their wedding, and (Caroline and John's cousin Maria Shriver, who is married to Arnold Schwarzenegger, was her maid of honor) and Caroline named their son John. John and Caroline were both at their mother's side constantly during her final days (Caroline visited and brought her children, John, Rose, and Tatiana, almost daily) and reportedly they still have dinner together at least once a week without fail.

John seems to be in almost constant touch with Caroline and they are both involved in each other's lives. A revealing moment occurred recently when John biked out to a New Jersey car dealership to look for a car. When the dealer offered to give John a ride back into town he refused the offer, telling the man that his sister could pick him up if he needed a ride. With all their fame and money, John and Caroline are exactly like all other sisters and brothers who depend on each other for the trivial necessities of life, like a ride home.

John at age five with the two most important women in his life. The family was vacationing on Baldy Mountain in Sun Valley, Idaho. PHOTO: PHOTOFEST

It is not overstatement to acknowledge that Jackie and Caroline are the two most important women in John Jr.'s life. He greatly loved and tenderly cared for his mother; he loves, respects, and is proud of his big sister. (Caroline feels the same about her brother and his achievements. She supports him personally and professionally and even loaned him an antique replica sword for the cover of his magazine, *George*.)

As probably the two most famous siblings in America, they are, in actuality, just a brother and sister who have had a life thrust upon them that could have brought lesser people to their knees.

In John and Caroline's case, it has simply made them stronger, and made the bond between brother and sister even greater.

SEVEN J.F.K. JR. POP CULTURE MOMENTS

John F. Kennedy Jr. has been in the spotlight since his birth and yet, it is as though he has been seen from a distance. Until recently, John hardly made any *scheduled* public appearances or comments, preferring to maintain a low profile and emulate his mother's lifelong insistence on privacy.

But there have been a few classic "moments" in the past couple of decades in which John was either the (willing) center of attention or the (unwilling) object of desire or speculation.

The Dedication of the John F. Kennedy Memorial Library, October 20, 1979

On a bright fall Saturday in 1979 in the Dorchester suburb of Boston, John F. Kennedy Jr., after being warmly introduced by his older sister Caroline, mounted the podium in front of the library built in honor of his father and began to read. John, who was eighteen at the time and who would turn nineteen a month later, read a poem by Stephen Spender that was intended as a tribute to the man they were all there to remember and praise.

The poem was, "I Think Continually of Those Who Were Truly Great," which begins:

> *I think continually of those who were truly great.*
> *Who, from the womb, remembered the soul's history*
> *Through corridors of light where the hours are suns,*
> *Endless and singing.*

Almost the entire Kennedy family was present at the dedication, including Jackie and Rose Kennedy. The day was primarily a tribute to the late President Kennedy, but John's cousin Joe, Robert Kennedy's son, was miffed that his father was not being honored with the same degree of acclaim as was being given to his Uncle Jack. Joe got up after John and gave an inflammatory speech,

John at yet another civic function. John attends so many of these affairs, you'd almost think he was a . . . politician! PHOTO: PHOTOFEST

attacking the banking and oil industries, and embarrassing President Jimmy Carter and many members of the family.

John and Caroline were silent following Joe's speech. They manifested their mother's restrained decorum and they did not publicly comment on cousin Joe's attempt to steal the spotlight away from their father.

John's Speech at the Democratic National Convention, July 1988

"Over a quarter of a century ago, my father stood before you to accept the nomination for the presidency of the United States," said John F. Kennedy Jr. at the July 1988 Democratic National Convention in Atlanta, Georgia. "So many of you came into public service because of him and in a very real sense it is because of you he is with us today."

John was only twenty-seven years old when he introduced his uncle Ted Kennedy at the Democratic Convention, but his poise, presence, and charisma belied his years.

Walter Isaacson of *Time* magazine remarked to Hendrik Hertzberg of The *New Republic* that when John ascended the podium, his astonishing good looks so impressed the audience that he felt the roof of the Omni Auditorium might buckle from the "sudden drop in air pressure caused by the simultaneous sharp intake of so many thousands of breaths."

Hertzberg wrote that John had a simple, quiet, and modest charm that served him exceptionally well before that partisan crowd and which also made quite an impression on the national television viewing audience. In fact, John's winning appeal prompted even a jaded newsman like Tom Brokaw to remark, "He is as charming and handsome as a movie star."

This appearance seemed to mark the start of a period in which John would have a more public persona, one in which he is perceived as being more mature and less of (as he had been described by some journalists) a superficial dilettante. Upon its conclusion, John's convention speech received a thundering, two-minute *standing* ovation. Republican consultant Richard Viguerie later said of John's speech, "I can't remember a word of the speech, but I do remember a good delivery. I think it was a plus for the Democrats and the boy. He is strikingly handsome."

At the convention, John's uncle, Senator Ted Kennedy, was asked what the chances were that John would join the "family business" of politics sometime down the line. Senator Kennedy responded that he believed that John would at some point get involved in public affairs. "Not necessarily running for office," he explained, "but trying to make some sort of contribution."

In addition to his memorable appearance and speech, this convention also marked John's very first political interview. After his speech, John was interviewed for NBC by journalist Connie Chung:

CONNIE CHUNG Tell me, that was your first time speaking before such a large audience, wasn't it?

JOHN F. KENNEDY JR. It was. I've done occasional campaign appearances with Teddy, but this was certainly the largest that I've ever seen.

CONNIE CHUNG And how did it feel?

JOHN F. KENNEDY JR. It felt pretty good, surprisingly.

CONNIE CHUNG Were you nervous at all?

JOHN F. KENNEDY JR. Yes. Right now. (Laughs) But it happened, you know? It's over. I knew it would be over soon. That's all I thought about really.

CONNIE CHUNG Tell me why you decided to do it.

JOHN F. KENNEDY JR. Because Teddy asked. That's enough.

CONNIE CHUNG Now you're . . . what year in law school are you at NYU?

JOHN F. KENNEDY JR. I'm finishing my last year.

CONNIE CHUNG Do you think you might be interested in going into politics?

JOHN F. KENNEDY JR. Well, I'm completely busy and consumed by what I'm doing right now. And obviously, I find public issues interesting and I can't help but find a convention like this interesting, but I'm just—you know, I'll see what happens and I'm happy doing what I'm doing.

CONNIE CHUNG One of your cousins, I think, Patrick, is a delegate from Rhode Island.

JOHN F. KENNEDY JR. Yeah.

CONNIE CHUNG Would you consider doing that maybe four years from now? Becoming a delegate?

JOHN F. KENNEDY JR. Gosh, I really can't think what I'm doing next year. What I'm doing in four years I really don't know. But I'll just have to see.

The *People* Magazine "Sexiest Man Alive" Issue, September 12, 1988

The funky, irreverent, blatantly panting biographical profile of John by Joyce Wadler in this "Sexiest Man Alive" issue began:

Okay, ladies, this one's for you—but first some ground rules. GET YOUR EYES OFF THAT MAN'S CHEST! He's a serious fellow. Third-year law student. Active with charities. Scion of the most charismatic family in American politics and heir to its most famous name.

She continues:

Get your eyes off that man's extraordinarily defined thighs! What do you think, he strips down to his shorts for a game of touch football in Central park so strangers can gape at them? They are fantastic, though. Measure three, four feet around. Legend has it that if he lived in Tahiti, instead of Manhattan, he could crack coconuts with them.

John on the dais with uncle Ted and mother Jackie. No political aspirations of his own as yet.
PHOTO: PHOTOFEST

Joyce Wadler then goes on to discuss John's "tushie," what he might look like naked, his ego, his partying style, his apartment, his style of dress, his intellect, and his possible political interests.

Friends of John's report that he was secretly flattered by *People*'s crowning of him as the "Sexiest Man," but that he had to endure merciless teasing because of it. Another result of the magazine's cover story was that now he was no longer simply an heir to Camelot, but rather had been transformed overnight into an American icon unto himself, a reluctant sex symbol at a time when he was trying to establish himself as someone worthy of the Kennedy name. Suddenly, he was a pin-up boy blinking in the bright glare of a million flashbulbs and he wasn't all too thrilled by the paparazzi and J.F.K. Jr. groupies who were now camping out outside his apartment building.

The "Sexiest Man" feature included (surprise) several sexy photos of John and was reportedly one of *People*'s best-selling issues.

Jackie was aghast at this blatantly provocative cover story but did not comment publicly on what she saw as an exploitative feature reeking of bad taste.

The Annual Profiles in Courage Award, Inaugurated 1990

In November 1989, John read and recorded his father's book *Profiles in Courage* for Caedmon Records on the condition that the record company make a large contribution to the John F. Kennedy Memorial Library.

Shortly thereafter, John and Caroline established the annual Profiles in Courage Award in memory of their father, an honor which would be bestowed on an individual who manifested great moral courage in the face of tremendous opposition, or who had performed some exemplary public service.

In early 1990, John made an eloquent and emotional statement about the establishment of the Award:

[A]ll his life, my father felt deeply about politics, that in fact it was an honorable profession. I think probably his proudest legacy is that, during the time he was president and in the years after he died, people who normally wouldn't have chosen a political career or involved themselves in politics, suddenly had a new feeling about politics and public service. Therefore, they got involved and committed themselves.

Throughout my life, people have come up to me and said, "I got into government because of your father." I feel great pride in that. So,
as my father tried to do in his book and in his life, we want to recognize and encourage not only excellence in public service but also rare courage: people who have sacrificed something, taken a position that is politically unpopular and stuck to it because it is the morally right thing to do . . .

My father believed deeply in the importance of politics and public service—that, in a democracy, it's one of the highest callings. So we want to encourage people to enter politics to serve their country. As many people as possible should be involved in political life—the more, the better. And when people don't care about the issues and decline to be involved, that can be a shame and a loss for the country.

President John F. Kennedy Jr. greeting his constituents? Not yet! Here he is in 1994, at a Worcester rally in support of his uncle Ted's re-election.
PHOTO: BROOKS KRAFT, SYGMA

Each year since the establishment of the award, John and Caroline have presented it to someone they felt was worthy of its acclaim.

In 1992, John and Caroline gave the award to maverick Connecticut Governor Lowell Weicker (who pushed through a needed income tax and ended up universally reviled and loathed by the residents of Connecticut) and in a rare television interview the morning of the award, Weicker spoke on national TV to four million viewers of *The Today Show*. (He said of the award, "[I]t's the type of recognition that makes everything worthwhile, that at least somebody knows what it is you were trying to do out there, even if maybe forty thousand people are coming down on your head.")

The winners of the award have been civil rights advocate Carl Elliott Sr. (1990); Georgia Supreme Court Justice Charles Weltner (1991); Connecticut Governor Lowell P. Weicker Jr. (1992); New Jersey Governor Jim Florio (1993); Chairman of the House Banking Committee, Congressman Henry Gonzalez (1994); Congressman Michael L. Synar (1995); and Georgia School Superintendent Dr. Corkin Cherubini (1996).

The *Seinfeld* Episodes, "The Contest" and "The Pilot, Part 2"

"The Contest"   This classic fourth season *Seinfeld* episode is one of the funniest installments of the series and without a doubt one of the all-time most hilarious half hours of television comedy ever broadcast. "The Contest" was written by *Seinfeld*'s cocreator Larry David and no fewer than five interwoven stories are brilliantly juggled and ultimately resolved.

The five plotlines are:
- George's chagrin at getting caught by his mother while masturbating to one of her *Glamour* magazines and his subsequent obsession with watching her sexy hospital roommate get a sponge bath.
- Jerry, Elaine, Kramer, and George's masturbation self-denial contest.
- Jerry's frustration over not being able to sleep with his new girlfriend Marla the Virgin.
- Kramer's fascination with a woman across the street from Jerry's apartment who parades around totally naked with the shades wide open.
- Elaine's futile attempt at getting a date with John F. Kennedy Jr.

The episode begins, as usual, with Jerry's monologue. He talks about the disgust he feels when he thinks about his parents having sex and says that if he ever found out that he was adopted he might not be too upset because then he could rest knowing that his parents had never had sex.

The first scene is in a booth in Monk's Diner. Jerry, Kramer, and Elaine discuss whether or not hostage takers holding someone prisoner would do their laundry for them. George comes in and says, "My mother caught me." He then explains that he was alone in his mother's house and one of her *Glamour* magazines got him excited and he started to "You know . . ." His mother walked in on him and screamed, "George! What are you doing? My God!," then tripped, fell, and ended up in the hospital in traction.

This whole incident so traumatized George that he says that he's never doing "it" again. No one believes him and they end up agreeing to a four-way contest of denial, with the one holding out longest winning the competition. Each of the gang bets $100, but they insist on "odds" from Elaine because they claim that it's easier for women not to do it. Jerry defends the male affection for this particular act by telling her it's part of their lifestyle and uses daily shaving as an example. Elaine tries to refute his argument by proclaiming that she shaves her legs, too, which Kramer chimes in with, "Not every day."

They finally agree on the financial terms; decide they will use the Honor System; and then link pinkys and swear to begin The Contest.

Later, back in Jerry's apartment, George talks on the phone with his mother. She is still in the hospital and insists that George see a psychiatrist. He refuses but tells her he'll be up to see her a little later. Jerry tells George that he has a date that evening with Marla the Virgin. When George asks how that's going, Jerry replies, "I've got my troops amassed across the border. I'm just waiting for someone to give me the go-ahead."

Kramer bursts in and announces that there is a naked woman in the apartment across the street. They all rush to the window to watch the woman walk around but then Kramer suddenly decides to leave. While he's gone, George and Jerry discuss what it must be like in a nudist colony. They finally decide that everyone—the chambermaids, the waiters, the gardener—are all nude, all the time: "One big Nude-O-Rama." Kramer returns, slams a pile of money down on the counter and announces, "I'm out."

The next scene takes place in Estelle Costanza's hospital room. George sits next to her bed as his mother berates him saying that she went out for a quart of milk and came home to find her son "treating his body like it was an amusement park!" Mrs. Costanza again tells George he should see a psychiatrist, and just as he's preparing to leave, a nurse comes in and announces that it's time for the woman in the next bed to get her nightly sponge bath. George is mesmerized by the nude curvaceous silhouette of the woman as the nurse bathes her, and he decides to stick around for a while.

Actress Jane Leeves, who played "The Virgin" on the hilarious J.F.K. Jr.-themed episode of *Seinfeld*, "The Contest." PHOTO: PHOTOFEST

The scene then shifts to the New York Health Club where Elaine is talking to her friend Joyce, who works at the club. Joyce says that Elaine will thank her for getting her in today because a certain someone is going to be in Elaine's class. When Joyce reveals that this person is John F. Kennedy Jr., Elaine goes into shock:

ELAINE: (*stunned*) In my class? John Kennedy's gonna be in *my* class?

JOYCE: I can get you a spot right behind him. He has got a *great butt*.

ELAINE: (*dazed*) Yeah. Butt, butt. Great butt. John-John's butt.

Meanwhile, Jerry and Marla are making out in the front seat of Jerry's car. Marla wants to slow down and Jerry agrees, telling her he doesn't care about the sex. They make a date for Saturday night and Jerry goes home.

We then see the first of the episode's "tossing and turning" scenes. Jerry, George, and Elaine all cannot sleep, but Kramer, however, is out like a light.

The next morning Jerry is morose and agitated. Kramer comes in and asks if he made it through the night, inquiring, "Are you still Master of Your Domain?" Jerry replies that he is indeed, but that he wants the woman across the street to pull down her shades. He can't take it anymore, he tells Kramer.

He can't convince himself to leave the house when the naked woman is home; he's dating a virgin; and he's in The Contest: "Something's gotta give!"

Kramer begs Jerry not to tell the woman to close her shades, Jerry relents, and Kramer sits by the window, waiting for her next appearance.

Later, at the diner, George tells Jerry about the daily sponge baths in his mother's hospital room and they discuss The Contest. Jerry asks George if he is still Master of his Domain and George tells him that he's King of the County. "You?" George asks. "Lord of the Manor," Jerry replies.

Elaine arrives and fills them in on her latest "adventure." She tells them that J.F.K. Jr. was in her aerobics class and that he worked out right in front of her. She also reveals that they actually had a conversation, Lame as it may have been:

ELAINE: I timed my walk to the door so we'd get there at the exact same moment. And he says to me, "Quite a workout."
GEORGE: "Quite a workout?" What did you say?
ELAINE: I said, "Yeah."
JERRY: Good one.

She also tells them that they shared a cab and that even though she was headed downtown, she went uptown just to spend time with John. After calming herself with a glass of ice water to her forehead, she assured Jerry and George that even though she was in a state of hyper-arousal from all this "John-John" contact, she was still "Queen of the Castle."

Later, George visits his mother at the hospital. She is surprised to see him again, but he tells her he's there because she's his mother, although the truth is that he wants to watch her roommate get a sponge bath. Mrs. Costanza asks him to go get her a sandwich but he refuses, because it's almost six-thirty: Showtime! George throws his mother some Tic-Tacs just as the nurse arrives for the bath.

At the same time, Elaine arrives at the New York Health Club for her evening workout (newly coifed and checking her breath) to learn that she missed John because he had taken the earlier class that day. Joyce did make Elaine's day, though, when she told her that she had made an impression on John and that he had asked about her and had wanted to know if she was single.

JOYCE: He said you were just his type.
ELAINE: Okay, are you trying to hurt me? Are you trying . . . you're trying to injure me, right? You're trying to hurt me.
JOYCE: He also told me to tell you he'll be in your neighborhood tomorrow around nine o'clock. So he's gonna stop in front of your building if you wanna come down and say hello. (*Elaine is in shock*).

Back in Jerry's apartment, Jerry is watching *Tiny Toons* on Nickelodeon and talking to his mother on the phone. Kramer, in the meantime, is sitting by the window watching the naked woman across the street. Jerry tries to take his mind off sex by singing, "The wheels of the bus go round and round, round and round," but Kramer sings along, changing the words to "The woman across the block has nothing on, nothing on."

We then see another "tossing and turning" bed scene, only this time, both Elaine and Kramer are sound asleep, while George and Jerry are still frustrated and wide awake.

The following morning, George and Jerry bicker over the coffee. George complains that all Jerry has is instant coffee and Jerry barks at him, "I don't keep real coffee in here! I get my coffee on the outside!"

Elaine buzzes up and while they're waiting for her, George accuses Jerry of stealing his socks. Elaine comes in, puts a pile of money down on the counter, signaling she is out of The Contest. "Oh, my God," Jerry exclaims. "The Queen is dead!" George asks her what happened and Elaine tells him, "It was John–John." Jerry and George both understand and say in unison, "Oh, John–John!" Elaine tells Jerry that she's meeting Kennedy out front of his building later and muses, "Elaine Benes Kennedy Jr."

A few hours later Jerry and Marla are making out on Jerry's couch. She finally tells him that she wants to go into the bedroom and even though he really wants to, he turns her down. Marla pushes for an explanation and he tells her about The Contest, which so outrages her that she storms out of the building where she runs into Elaine waiting for John-John. Marla hails a cab and tells Elaine that she wants nothing to do any more with her or her "perverted friends."

Back in Jerry's apartment, Jerry tells Elaine that when he told Marla about their Contest, she stormed out. George arrives and gives Elaine the devastating news that John had shown up downstairs and driven off with Marla the Virgin. Jerry, George, and a crushed Elaine are shocked when they look across the street and see Kramer waving at them from inside the Naked Woman's apartment.

We then see the final "tossing and turning" scene only this time no one is awake: Elaine, Jerry, and George are all sound asleep, as is Kramer, only he's in bed with the Naked Woman.

The episode ends with a shot of Marla the No-Longer-a-Virgin in bed with the John F. Kennedy Jr. character. "Oh, John," she whispers, "that was wonderful!"

During his closing monologue, Jerry talks about how much men want to see women naked.

"The Pilot, Part 2"   This fourth season episode was the coda to "The Contest" and actually featured "John F. Kennedy Jr." commenting on Jerry and George's pilot episode of their new sitcom, *Jerry*, while at home in bed with Marla the Virgin (again played by *Frasier*'s Jane Leeves).

Part 2 of the "The Pilot" (it was a two-part episode) focused on the shooting of Jerry and George's new NBC show. After a raucous half hour filled with all manner of outlandish scenarios, including stolen raisins, a constipated Kramer, and a restaurant that only hires large-breasted women, everyone gathers to watch the airing of the pilot episode of *Jerry*.

Denizens from past *Seinfeld* episodes all make an appearance, including George's lesbian ex-girlfriend; the old man with the record collection; the Drake and the Drakette; the Chinese food delivery guy George persuaded to call China for hair-growing cream; the kid in the bubble; Jerry's parents; Calvin Klein; Jerry's date with the "spectacular" breasts (played by Teri Hatcher); a sound-asleep Newman; and John F. Kennedy Jr. and Marla the Virgin.

The J.F.K. Jr. scene takes place in a bedroom. Marla is lying in bed while John is sitting at the end of the bed on the edge of the mattress with the remote in his hand watching *Seinfeld*. He is wearing a blue robe and we see everything of him except his face. During the show, Marla and John have the following conversation:

MARLA THE VIRGIN: John, what are you doing? Come back to bed.

JOHN F. KENNEDY JR.: This show looks interesting. Isn't he that Seinfeld fellow you went out with?

MARLA THE VIRGIN: Ooh, he's horrible, horrible!

JOHN F. KENNEDY JR.: Nevertheless . . .

The funniest thing about this "J.F.K. Jr." scene is the voice they gave to his character. Rather than try for something even remotely like John Kennedy's actual voice, the *Seinfeld* folks opted for an exaggerated Boston accent, resulting in a rather nasally voice that sounded exactly like . . . John's father, John F. Kennedy *Sr.* No credit was given for the actor who voiced the Kennedy character and John himself didn't appear in either one of the *Seinfeld* episodes.

One hopes John Jr. found all this amusing.

J.F.K. Jr.'s Appearance on *Murphy Brown*, September 18, 1995

On Monday, September 18, 1995, John F. Kennedy Jr. appeared as himself in a one-and-a-half minute scene in the eighth-season premiere of Candice Bergen's CBS sitcom, *Murphy Brown*.

There is a running joke on the show that Murphy can't keep her secretaries, and there's a new one at the desk almost every week. John first appears sitting at the secretary's desk. He has his back to the audience and Murphy lets loose, in her inimitable way, on this newcomer, someone she perceives as just another useless cretin from the *FYI* secretarial pool.

But then she realizes who *this one* is, and he tells her why he's there.

This episode, which was taped on Friday, August 11, 1995, had a live audience that had not been told who the "special guest" was going to be. Candice Bergen later told *TV Guide*, "I haven't heard so many women screaming since the Beatles. I had to wait quite a while to deliver my line."

Regarding his appearance on the successful show, John issued a statement in which he said, "We wanted to introduce the magazine to as many people as possible in unexpected ways. People always ask how we're going to make politics fun. *Murphy Brown* allows us to do that."

The show's executive producer Bill Diamond reported that working with John was "a breeze," but an inside source on the show told *TV Guide* that *George*'s Editor-in-Chief had very specific ideas—and demands—about how his appearance would be handled: "He spent hours discussing the promos for the show with the [studio] people. Somebody said dealing with him was like trying to get concessions from the Pope."

Another source told the magazine what John was like on the set: "He was very cool, very friendly, and unimpressed with himself. He looked just like another regular guy in khakis and a golf shirt. There were no bodyguards, no entourage."

TV Guide also reported an incident that truly illustrates the fascination and mystique surrounding J.F.K. Jr. It seems that John decided to work out in the TV studio's gym after an afternoon rehearsal. "That sort of lit up the phone lines around here," a Warner Bros. staffer told the magazine's Mike Hammer. "All of a sudden, everybody felt like using the weight room."

George editor John Kennedy Jr. surprises Murphy Brown with a special magazine cover made up just for her. Murphy is less than thrilled with his gift and John storms out offended. John performed his scene flawlessly and caused quite a stir at the studio the day of the taping.
PHOTO: PHOTOFEST

This is the scene from *Murphy Brown* in which John made his primetime network acting debut:

MURPHY BROWN: (*entering newsroom*) Oh, Hi. I'm Murphy Brown. You must be my new secretary.

JOHN F. KENNEDY JR.: (*sitting at secretary's desk*) Oh, Murphy, hi!

MURPHY BROWN: John, hi! I guess the whole lawyer thing didn't work out? That's a tough break. Would you file this for me? (*hands him a stack of papers*).

JOHN F. KENNEDY JR.: Actually, Murphy, I was just writing you a note. I came over to bring you this wedding present, but they told me that the whole thing had been called off, so, uh . . .

MURPHY BROWN: This is how rumors get started! (*grabs present*). A present for me! You Kennedys are so thoughtful and generous! (*Rips open package*) Wonder what it is?

JOHN F. KENNEDY JR.: I think you're really gonna like it.

MURPHY BROWN: (*takes out magazine*) What the hell is this?

JOHN F. KENNEDY JR.: It's a copy of *George*. It's a new political magazine I'm editing. I had the guys in the art department mock up a cover with you on it. It's pretty great, huh?

MURPHY BROWN: (*rummaging through the tissue paper*) That's it?

JOHN F. KENNEDY JR.: No, no. There's a one-year free subscription with a card!

MURPHY BROWN: (*sarcastically*) Gee, I hope you didn't have to sell the compound.

JOHN F. KENNEDY JR.: Okay, fine, if that's your attitude, but don't come crying to me when you have to pay full newsstand price! (*storms out of office*)

J.F.K. Jr. on *Oprah*

As we have seen over the years, John Jr. rarely talks to the press. We have not yet seen John sitting for a cryfest with Barbara Walters on *20/20*, nor have we watched him stroll the beaches of Hyannis Port with Ed Bradley for an installment of *60 Minutes*.

John's uncle, Senator Ted Kennedy and his wife, arriving at the Special Olympics in New Haven in 1995.
PHOTO: ANNMARIE LEVATINO

It was quite the media event, then, when John agreed to be interviewed by talk show queen Oprah Winfrey, especially since he consented to be her sole guest for an entire hour on her syndicated show.

On Tuesday, September 3, 1996, John Jr., nattily dressed in a dark blue suit (that he said he wore "special" for Oprah) and a patterned tie, sat down for a forty-five minute interview with Oprah.

An almost-apoplectic Oprah introduced John by saying, "He is here! Everything you ever thought, you ever heard, you ever read about John F. Kennedy Jr., he is all that, and then some." John entered to an overwhelming standing ovation by the studio audience and could be heard commenting to Oprah, "Wow, you do this every day!" Oprah (who kept annoyingly interrupting John during his responses throughout the entire interview) then thanked him for coming on and admitted that she had wanted him to be the first to sit in her new chairs (her set had been redesigned over the summer hiatus), playfully telling John she was thrilled to get *his* "behind" in her chair.

John and Oprah first chatted briefly about John's sister Caroline's previous appearances on Oprah's show and Oprah gushed that she was flattered to learn that John had actually watched her program.

Here is a selection of a few interesting remarks made by John during the show:

On his much-televised argument with Carolyn Bessette in a New York park:

Obviously I was a little surprised when the whole thing happened, but [intense media coverage] kind of comes and goes. I think ultimately . . . people realize that one's private moments are probably best kept private.

On whether or not John, as a public figure, has a right to privacy and, by the way, does he actually have any?:

I've got a little bit. I've got enough. I think that [Caroline and I] are used—to a certain degree—of being watched and I think that you're [always] aware of it even if you're not *consciously* aware of it. I understand that there's interest and, certainly, that interest has given both of us great opportunities, so I can't complain too much. Sometimes I wish it wasn't always that way, but then you wouldn't have invited me on your show! (Laughs)

After Robert Kennedy's assassination, it would be fair to say that uncle Ted became somewhat of a surrogate father figure for John and Caroline. PHOTO: ANN-MARIE LEVATINO

On whether or not he feels that his magazine *George* is successful just because his name is attached to it:

As far as readers, readers might have bought the first one, and maybe even the second one but we're now doing our seventh issue and I don't think people would have stuck with us if we weren't somehow delivering.

On his family's reaction to his infamous "Marilyn" *George* cover:

I think my family is used to all manner of controversy so I think—in the grand scheme of things—this probably didn't register too high on the Richter scale.

On the pressure to make something of himself because of his family's enormous reputation and their role in American culture and history:

There *is* this great weight of expectation and anticipation and I think that part of you wants to sort of address that in some way, maybe do something different, but just to sort of engage it. . . . It was the thing of having a fulfilling life and the other stuff sort of takes care of itself, I think.

John adjusts his tie as he enters the VIP area at the Special Olympics in New Haven in 1995. PHOTO: ANNMARIE LEVATINO

Oprah then asked John how he ended up being so normal. John replied, "I feel this is a segue leading to talking about my mother somehow," and the talk did then turn to Jackie. Oprah asked John if he thought his mother would be happy about his appearance on her show and John responded, "I think [in] the days leading up to it, she'd be a little circumspect, but then after it, she'd be very happy about it."

Oprah then poignantly revealed to John that his mother, Jackie, was the one interview she had dreamed of getting all her professional life but that after his mother died, Oprah was glad that she had never succeeded in interviewing her. The talk then turned to Jackie's lifelong refusal to grant media interviews and John explained, "It was not really a studied decision on her part; it was just that her life was easier if she lived it privately. And once you start answering those questions, then where do you stop, really? So for her, it was a practical consideration and it made more sense for her."

A powerful and stunning moment occurred during the interview as John was commenting on Kennedy family pictures that were being projected on a screen behind him and Oprah. The two talked about John playing under his father's desk and boating off Hyannis Port, and John looked up at each slide as it appeared. But then the famous picture of John saluting during his father's funeral procession appeared and John immediately turned away from the screen. In a bit of a lapse, Oprah, instead of picking up on John's discomfort, insensitively talked about that "horrible November" and asked John if he remembered that moment and also asked him why he had made that famous salute. John picked at some lint on his pant leg and said simply, "I really don't remember." Oprah pressed on, however, asking him if he *really* didn't remember that whole day and John just mumbled an acknowledgment that no, he really didn't remember. The moment was uncomfortable and, thankfully, Oprah then went to a commercial. This whole episode illustrated that even though the Kennedys have become cultural and political icons and archetypes in America, they are still members of a *family*, and they can still hurt at being reminded of an unbearably tragic loss.

Back from the commercial, Oprah fawned over John a bit (calling him "perfectly charming") and they then talked about the new "20 Most Fascinating Women in Politics" issue of *George* that was then on the newsstands. From there, the discussion moved to John's interview with George Wallace in the first issue of *George*.

More from John:

On whether or not anyone intimidated him:
(To Oprah) Yeah, you do. (Laughs)

On whether or not John will ever run for office:
I've certainly thought about it . . . I really grew up in a political environment, going to fundraisers, seeing that stuff and it was important to [me to] really do something different. John Adams said that you should become a politician at the *end* of your life when you bring a wealth of life experience to bear on that office. For me, I think I was eager to try something different, to see another part of life . . . and I had an idea to be an entrepreneur.

His response to the Sothebys auction of some of his parents' possessions:
I was a little taken aback. We didn't really know what to expect, and it was obviously a very difficult set of decisions that went into creating that. We kept the things that really mattered to us. So you can keep the things that matter to you, you have to get rid of other things. My mother kept *every single thing* that she ever got in her life and either we were going to open up a museum, or we were going to have more normal lives. We have the things that really matter and really were valued, and really were evocative of our mother, and that's what's important.

On whether or not his sister Caroline bosses him around:
(Laughs) She used to, but now, it's a little more even!

On his sister Caroline's influence on him:
(Laughs) She's the older sister, you know? We're obviously very close and as a younger brother, you look up to your sister. I was the man of the family, as it were, and it was sort of the three of us, and now [it's] the two of us, and I feel so lucky that I have such a close relationship with her.

The hour was coming to a close and Oprah asked John a couple of final questions, including, "Do you feel happy?", to which a good-natured John winningly responded, "When? Always?" Oprah clarified that she meant "in general" and John assured her that he did, indeed feel happy. Oprah then told him that the reason she asked him that was because "We Americans want to believe . . . we want John-John to be happy!"

John explained that his magazine *George* gave him a great sense of fulfillment and that he felt very lucky to be doing something he loved. When asked what he did for fun, John said he ran around, went to plays a lot, and Roller-bladed.

Oprah then thanked John (who could be seen telling her "That was really fun!") and went to a commercial. After the commercial, Oprah (who kept reminding John throughout the interview that she was very close friends with his cousin Maria Shriver) talked to the audience about John, again describing him as charming and asking them, "Didn't his mother raise a nice son?"

Oprah then revealed that she had refused to ask John when he was getting married because that was the number one question people were always asking *her*, and she felt that John's answer was really nobody's business but John's.

Eighteen days later, John and Carolyn Bessette were wed in a small ceremony on Cumberland Island, Georgia.

Oprah did not attend the ceremony. One wonders whether she was invited.

SIX J.F.K. JR. SCANDALS

Okay, so maybe "scandal" is too strong a word, but it got your attention and it makes the point that there have been a few episodes and situations in John Jr.'s life that have served as fodder for the gossip columnists and tabloid reporters, and which have occasionally shown a side of John that he may not be too thrilled about the public being aware of.

The Secret Nude Photos

I can sense the ladies (and not a few men, I would guess) salivating already: Yes, full frontal nude photos of John F. Kennedy Jr. exist, although they have not (yet) been published.

Shortly after his thirtieth birthday in 1990, John vacationed on the island of St. Bart's in the French West Indies where he swam and walked around on Governor's Beach completely naked. A New York travel agent named Shelby Shusteroff who was also vacationing there, recognized him and took his picture. She has reportedly refused huge amounts of money for the nude pictures. Several people have acknowledged being shown the shots in private. Ms. Shusteroff has said that the pictures were *not* taken for financial gain (apparently just for her own delight).

Following this incident, many people correctly noted that John probably should have known better. Twenty years earlier in 1971, John's mother Jackie was clandestinely photographed while sunbathing naked on Aristotle Onassis's private island Skorpios. Feeling totally secure, Jackie took off her suit and sunbathed in the raw, not knowing that a team of ten photographers stationed on a boat off the coast of the island were using powerful telescopic lenses and underwater cameras to snap her picture. These photographs were published in the Italian magazine *Playmen* and were later picked up by other magazines throughout the world. After this incident, Ari Onassis is reported to have said to friends, "She looks so lovely without clothes. Just look at that figure. I think I'll get an artist to paint her. She makes all the other nude ladies look like a bag of bones."

John may very well be asking here, "You've got pictures of what!?" John's life has been spent under a microscope and yet he still finds ways to laugh it all off! PHOTO: PHOTOFEST

John romps in the surf over a recent Labor Day weekend at the Kennedy compound in Hyannis Port. PHOTO: LAURA CAVANAUGH, GLOBE PHOTOS INC.

Whether or not the nude photographs of John will ever be published remains to be seen. Shusteroff has been steadfast in her refusal to sell them and yet, things happen. Unless she burns the pictures and the negatives, there is always a chance that someday they will appear in print.

Since John's nude romp on Governor's Beach, no one has reported catching him naked, although he has been shirtless in public many times in the past few years. He has, however, apparently kept his pants on (at least while in the public eye).

An interesting incident involving another episode of John swimming in the nude took place in 1966—when John was only six years old. This episode seemed to predict John's nude beach stroll twenty-three years later.

Jackie, John, and Caroline spent the 1966 Easter holiday in Argentina on the cattle ranch of the country's foreign minister Miguel Carcano. During their stay, John went swimming naked in a small stream on Carcano's ranch. Even then the media were watching John and Caroline like hawks and the next day, newspapers around the world ran a story headlined, "JFK Jr. Takes Dip in the Nude."

It's a twisted world indeed when a six-year-old boy jumping into a stream without a bathing suit is perceived as news, wouldn't you agree?

John's Reported Drinking and Drug Use

The focus of this feature might lead you to believe that this is going to be a recounting of scandalous and salacious episodes of drug usage and drunken binges, but the truth is that, like a lot of people, John drinks moderately; and friends and people who have been in his company confirm that he has also used marijuana and cocaine.

John likes tequila and beer and used to drink Scotch straight out of the bottle when he was fifteen and staying on Aristotle Onassis's island of Skorpios. Once, when John was twelve, he got caught drinking at Madison Square Garden with a friend. According to Wendy Leigh, the reporter never realized that John Kennedy Jr. was one of the kids who had gotten caught and so John's name never appeared in the papers. John's college roommates at Brown University have told stories of John's car often being loaded with empty beer cans. Today he frequents New York sports bars and restaurants but there are never reports of him being loud or leaving a place drunk. John's legendary good manners are reportedly always in evidence, even after he's had a few.

John seemed to develop a taste for marijuana when he was in his early teens and attending Collegiate in New York. John's classmate Wilson McCray told biographer Wendy Leigh, "[W]e were always getting caught for getting stoned." McCray also revealed that he and John used to smoke pot in the bathroom of Jackie's apartment, and also on the roof of her building.

John also smoked pot at Phillips Academy (as did many other students on campus at the time) and once got caught by campus security. He did not deny he had been smoking pot. His mother was greatly concerned that he would acquire a reputation for drug use as had many of his Kennedy cousins who were into drugs much deeper than John. Classmates who knew John at the time say he was just trying to fit in with the rest of the students and that he really wasn't a serious druggie. The Secret Service was still guarding him during this period and they apparently knew what was going on but didn't confront him about it.

The story is also told that as soon as Jackie left John's eighteenth birthday party at Le Club, John and his Andover buddies fired up joints and stayed at the club smoking and drinking until four in the morning. When they left the club, they were confronted by a photographer for the *National Enquirer*. A melee erupted and John ended up on the ground. His picture ended up in the papers because of this incident.

Through 1983, John continued to smoke pot and more than one source confirmed that he used cocaine for a while. But as Wendy Leigh described John's shift away from this lifestyle, "Despite those experiences, and the reckless seam that ran deep through the Kennedy nature, he had a powerful inner compass that ultimately steered him away from excess."

An interesting footnote to the chronicle of John's flirtation with soft drugs is that his sister Caroline was also no stranger to getting high. There is a story that Caroline once got caught growing pot in her mother's vegetable garden at Hyannis Port, and that John used to smoke Caroline's homegrown weed with her.

John's Appearance at the William Kennedy Smith Rape Trial

There was talk that John most decidedly did *not* want to make a high-profile appearance at his cousin William Kennedy Smith's rape trial, but that he bowed to the relentless pressures of his family, and did show up, even though it seemed as though he was uncomfortable sitting in the courtroom during testimony.

Acquitted rape suspect William Kennedy Smith is John's first cousin and one of his best friends. Here Willie arrives at the Special Olympics in New Haven in 1995. PHOTO: ANN-MARIE LEVATINO

A Kennedy employee named Jim Connor denied that there was any truth to that rumor when he said, "There was talk that Jackie had forced [John] to come, but that wasn't true. John is his own person and he came down because he wanted to help Willie."

The truth is probably somewhere in between.

John's first cousin and close friend William Kennedy Smith (the son of J.F.K.'s sister Jean) was charged with the rape of a young woman named Patricia Bowman. Smith met Bowman in 1991 on Good Friday evening at Au Bar, a chic Palm Beach watering hole frequented by people like the Kennedys and Ivana Trump.

Patricia Bowman said that Smith invited her back to the Kennedy Palm Beach compound and she admitted that she went willingly. She claimed that while the two of them were strolling on the beach, Smith suddenly stripped naked and went for a swim in the ocean. She said she then decided it was time to leave but that when she attempted to get to her car, Smith grabbed her and raped her near an outdoor swimming pool.

During the live broadcasting of the trial, Patricia Bowman's face was masked by a blue dot, although her identity would soon be revealed.

John spent five days in Florida attending the trial and was seen having lunch with Willie Smith and the defense team during his stay.

After what seemed like a decent interval and a fair modicum of support, John left for New York before the verdict was reached. William Kennedy Smith was ultimately acquitted of sexual battery, Florida's term for felony rape.

John's presence at the trial may or may not have made a difference in the verdict, but it illustrated his fierce and unwavering family loyalty. John made one final statement about how he felt about his family when he sent attorney Raoul Felder an enormous bouquet of yellow chrysanthemums. Felder had

**Adonis rising:
Bathing suit shots
are a favorite of the
photographers who
capture every move
John makes! And
for good cause—
they sell very well!
Imagine what those
nude pix would go
for!?** PHOTOS:
LAURA CAVANAUGH,
GLOBE PHOTOS

proclaimed on the tabloid TV show *A Current Affair* that cousin Willie's trial signified "the fall of the House of Kennedy." John's card to Felder that accompanied the flowers read, "Still standing, baby. Best, The House of Kennedy."

The Hunk Flunks: J.F.K. Jr. and the Bar Exam

John failed the New York Bar exam—twelve hours, 250 multiple choice questions, six essay questions—two times in a row.

The first time he failed, Stanley Chess, president of the BAR/BRI bar review course, published in *Newsweek* an article masquerading as an open letter to John, advising him how to pass the test the next time he took it. The magazine the *New Republic* called Chess's "letter" a blatant attempt at self-aggrandizement and promotion for his company, noting, "One looked in vain for the 'Paid Advertisement' warning on *Newsweek's* story about John F. Kennedy Jr.'s failing the New York bar exam last week."

John first took the exam in July 1989. He was one of 6,854 lawyers taking the test. He was one of 2,189 who failed.

In February 1990, he tried again. This time, he scored a 589 out of the required 600 points needed to pass. This failing was the one that generated the notorious *New York Post* headline, "The Hunk Flunks."

He tried one more time on Tuesday, July 24, 1990. This time he passed, learning the good news before work on Wednesday, November 7, 1990.

The embarrassment was over, and John was able to keep his job in the Manhattan District Attorney's office.

The Brawl in the Park

The March 12, 1996, issue of the *National Enquirer* featured a screaming cover headline that read "JFK ATTACKS LIVE-IN LOVER: Brutal bust-up leaves number-one hunk sobbing alone on the sidewalk." There was also a large photo of John and Carolyn Bessette shouting at each other; and an inset photo of Carolyn with her arm around John's neck.

Basically, what seems to have been a routine spat between two lovers turned into a scandalous, worldwide story simply because one of the combatants was John F. Kennedy Jr.

The *Enquirer's* story began, "In an astonishing in-your-face public fight, John F. Kennedy Jr. and his live-in love screamed, pushed and shoved each other as they fought over her engagement ring and their dog."

John and Carolyn Bessette were walking together in a New York park on Sunday, February 25, 1996 when the fireworks began. Unfortunately, they were being trailed by a photographer and an amateur videographer who both recorded the whole thing, including John sitting on a curb and supposedly weeping openly as Carolyn tried to comfort him.

The fight took place on a Sunday morning and it included Carolyn grabbing John around his neck, the two of them shouting in each other's faces, pushing and shoving, John ripping an emerald and diamond "friendship" ring off Carolyn's finger, and John pushing Carolyn in the face.

After the initial blow-up, the two of them sat on a park bench and fumed. At one point a little girl approached John and asked if she could pet his dog. He was charming and smiled at her. (Author Nellie Bly said that this was Jackie's training "kicking in.") As soon as the little girl left, though, the chilliness returned. Carolyn and John then got up and started walking home together, but it wasn't long before they began arguing again. At that point, John sat down on a curb and appeared to be publicly weeping as people passed by him. During this time, Carolyn berated him and appeared to be shouting at him as cars and people passed by.

The *Enquirer* reported that eyewitnesses said their shouted conversation included Carolyn demanding, "Give it to me!," and John shouting, "You've got your ring—you're not getting my dog!" John also exclaimed to Carolyn, "I don't even know the girl!" (His lips could easily be read on the videotape which aired on *Day & Date*.) Finally, Carolyn stormed off and John followed her, looking dejected and downtrodden.

John and Carolyn finally cooled down and ultimately walked off together; at first John following, but then the two of them stopping (after Carolyn broke away to light a cigarette) and embracing.

The *Day & Date* Video

As previously mentioned, John and Carolyn's argument was videotaped by paparazzi and aired on the CBS magazine show, *Day & Date* as "Sunday in the Park with John."

The tabloid show prolonged the agony by airing bits of the eighteen-minute tape for an entire week, with each segment augmented by comments from author Nellie Bly, John's cousin, author John Davis, *Daily News* columnist George Rush, and Jeannette Walls from *Esquire*.

Day & Date guests recklessly speculated as to the cause of the fight, suggesting that it was because John had made overtures to O.J. Simpson's ex-girlfriend Paula Barbieri and that Carolyn had found out about it; that Carolyn had revealed to John that she was pregnant, John had proposed, and Carolyn had turned him down; and that Carolyn wanted to make their relationship permanent and John had said no.

Walls said that John was very upset about the video; and she made the incredible claim that John was "eyeing a public office," and that this video was bad for his public image. She also claimed that John was linked with Claudia Schiffer and that Carolyn was upset about that.

Day & Date contacted John at the *George* office but John refused to talk about the fight.

Official Comment There were no formal statements from John or his camp but a few days after this incident, John was an unexpected guest on the *Howard Stern* radio program. Of course Stern asked him if he had seen the video that *Day & Date* was airing of him and Carolyn. John said that he didn't need to see it; he was in it.

Essentially, this was an embarrassing moment magnified because of John's celebrity status into a regrettable public airing of dirty laundry. George Rush spoke with Caroline Kennedy about the spat and she said, "It's private. I don't want to talk about it. John's doing fine."

According to *Day & Date*'s phone-in viewer poll, his fans agree:

Results of the *Day & Date* J.F.K. Jr. Telephone Poll:
Do you think the tape will hurt J.F.K.'s image?

NO: 87 percent
YES: 13 percent
Do you still think J.F.K. Jr. is the sexiest man alive?

YES: 77 percent
NO: 23 percent

Hard Copy

This outrageous piece—titled "Mystery Illness" and aired nationally on Wednesday, March 6, 1996— exemplifies everything celebrities hate about tabloid television and makes you wonder how the people who put this stuff together can sleep at night.

The segment began as follows:

Once crowned "Sexiest Man Alive," John F. Kennedy Jr. looks the picture of health, but tonight there are reports he may be battling a deadly disease similar to the one that affected his famous father.

The narration went on to suggest that beneath John's healthy exterior lies a "secret" disease that only his family knows about.

The ubiquitous Nellie Bly, shameless tabloid TV shill and author of *The Kennedy Men*, speculated wildly that John has postponed marriage because he has Addison's disease and he wants to live each day to the fullest before settling down. She talked about John's twenty pound weight loss in 1995 (that was attributed to a hyperactive thyroid) and extrapolated from this all kinds of disastrous health consequences for John.

You have to give *Hard Copy* credit: The piece was carefully written and meticulously hedged. Throughout the segment, the reporters and interview subjects used phrases such as "there are reports," and "it is being reported" but never said who previously reported as "facts" *Hard Copy's* wild conjectures.

The reporter interviewed "medical expert" Max Gomez who pontificated about how the disease was extremely serious and stated that Addison's could be fatal. Apparently *Hard Copy* could not get a *medical* doctor to come on the show and participate in their sensationalistic theorizing—their renowned "Dr." Gomez holds a Ph.D., *not* an M.D.

Nellie Bly then tells viewers that one of the "darkest secrets" of Jack Kennedy's life was his battle with Addison's disease. She speculates that it is "likely" that John is taking cortisone and that the mood swings that are sometimes a side effect of this drug could be responsible for the recent brawl in the park between him and Carolyn.

New York Post gossip columnist Cindy Adams then made an appearance and solemnly told the audience:

> *It would appear that John F. Kennedy, who has been handed the world on a silver platter, is not a very happy man. He seems to be in not robust health.*

"Dr." Gomez came back on to tell viewers that Addison's is treatable with cortisol (a hormone replacement drug) even if the patient is "almost on death's doorstep." The segment ended with the reporter announcing gravely that John may be facing his "toughest struggle yet."

"Mystery Illness" had a tone that bordered on hysteria and its obvious intention was to make people believe that John not only had Addison's disease but that he was seriously ill from it and that the drug therapy he was undergoing to treat the disease was turning him into a raging maniac.

The Kennedys acknowledge that John is being treated for a hyperactive thyroid, a condition that is *not* Addison's disease, although there are similarities. It seems as though *Hard Copy* took this fact, added the brawl in the park, came to some conclusions impossible to confirm without John's participation, and then aired a highly inflammatory, melodramatic, and recklessly speculative piece in order to milk the public's interest in John's argument with Carolyn for every rating point they could squeeze out of it.

Like we said, you have to wonder how these people sleep at night.

The catalog was beautiful; the array of possessions, awe-inspiring, and yet, the media was all over John and Caroline, accusing them of trying to "cash in" on their parents' memories.

Even the usually shameless comedienne Joan Rivers took umbrage at the decision to hold the auction. After the first session on April 23, 1996, though, she changed her mind about the whole thing, telling *USA Today*, "At first I thought it was terrible, what the family did. But I realized it's really nice. A lot of people, including my cousin Charlotte, can be walking around saying, 'I'm wearing something Jackie wore.' " Later Rivers announced plans to reproduce on scarves a painting she bought during the auction and sell the scarves on QVC. (The Friday, April 19, 1996 preview of the Jackie auction was delayed when Sotheby's received a bomb threat at about 2:45 that afternoon. The building was evacuated and searched but nothing was found.)

As is often the case in high-profile, celebrity-focused situations like this, however, the truth was quite different from the perception.

When Jackie learned she was dying she began to give great thought to the disposition of her estate.

Shortly before the auction, Pierre Salinger former Kennedy White House Press Secretary appeared on "Larry King Live" and discussed the auction:

LARRY KING: What do you think of this whole concept?

PIERRE SALINGER: I've done a lot of looking into it because I think it's important to understand why it's being done. And what I've discovered is that before Jackie died she came up with this idea and talked to her children about it, but she said it was going to be their final decision. [S]he felt she had to do this because, you know, when you die and you've got a lot of money, you have to pay tremendous taxes in the United States, and at least a very significant part of this sale is going to go to estate tax . . . but obviously, some of it will go to the children. But the other thing that she felt very strongly about was that some of these things had to go to the Kennedy Library. And there are absolutely incredible documents and archives and things like that that have gone to the Kennedy Library, including her wedding dress.

The first day of the auction, Salinger reiterated that this was not a callous "selling-off" of their parents' possessions, telling *USA Today*, "It was Jackie's original idea. She talked to her lawyers and had a meeting with John and Caroline and convinced them. By selling these things and paying the estate taxes, they're able to keep her big houses."

John and Caroline donated a great many items from Jackie's estate to the

A classic 1962 photo of Jackie, showing her wearing her famous three-strand simulated pearl necklace and a pair of diamond earrings, both of which were auctioned off by Sotheby's after her death. PHOTO: PHOTOFEST

John F. Kennedy Memorial Library, including 4,500 photographs; 38,000 pages of documents; and 200 works of art and other artifacts.

Items Belonging to, Used by, or Associated With John Jr. That Were Auctioned Off

The Jackie Onassis auction was the single highest-grossing sale in the history of Sotheby's.

Officials at Sotheby's had conservatively estimated the auction would gross around $5 million. That estimate was thrown out the window when on the very first day bidding brought in a record-breaking $4.5 million. By the end of the second day, after a total of 453 lots had been auctioned off, the take was up to almost $21 million. The final total (including the buyer's premium) for all 1,195 lots was $34,461,495 (an average of $28,838 per lot).

J.F.K.'s rocking chair (appraised value, $3,000-$5,000) sold for $442,500; a walnut humidor given to J.F.K. by Milton Berle (appraised value, $2,000-$2,500) was the first evening's highest-ticket item selling for $574,500 to Marvin Shanken, publisher of *Cigar Aficionado* magazine. The humidor has an engraved plaque on it that reads, "To J.F.K. Good Health—Good Smoking, Milton Berle—1/20/61." Milton Berle, bidding on the phone from his home in Los Angeles, wanted to get the humidor back for his own collection but was outbid by Shanken.

Lot 33 "A Victorian Mahogany Youth Chair, probably French, second half 19th Century." This 38-inch wooden high chair was estimated to be worth between $1,500 and $2,000 and was described as having a "tub-shaped backrest with red velvet upholstery, and with straight arms, basket footrest, sliding tray and molded cabriole legs." This was John's high chair when he lived with his parents at the White House. It was put up for bid in the first session of the auction, Tuesday, April 23, 1996, at 7:30 P.M. After frenzied bidding, the chair ultimately sold for the astonishing price of **$85,000.**

Lot 50 This was the printed program from the dedication of the Runnymede Memorial in Great Britain that was attended by the entire First Family. It was priced at between $1,500 and $2,000 and included a photo of John and Caroline walking with their mother at Runnymede. This program was also offered in the first session of the auction and it sold for **$34,500.**

Lot 454 A "Simulated Pearl Necklace." This 19-inch triple strand of one hundred thirty-nine, 9–9.5 millimeter simulated pearls was one of the most sought after pieces in the auction. Its value was estimated at between $500 and $700 (extremely high for simulated pearls) and its appeal stemmed from a very famous photo of Jackie wearing these pearls and holding two-year-old John in her arms (taken at the White House in August 1962), while John tugs on one of the strands.

In an interview with *USA Today*, Rebecca Knapp of *Art & Antiques* magazine summed up the appeal of this unique piece of jewelry both valueless and priceless at the same time: "Not only is it Jackie's pearls, but John–John touched them." The pearls ended up selling for **$211,500.** The buyer was the Franklin Mint. Jack Wilkie, a spokesperson for the Mint, said they would display the necklace in its museum and stores and that they also planned on making copies of the pearls for sale.

Footnote On Monday, April 29, 1996, former First Lady Barbara Bush spoke at Lincoln Center at a benefit for Literacy Partners. Bush, who popularized the three-strand simulated pearl choker look during her stint in the White House, publicly acknowledged that she got the look from Jackie, specifically the strand auctioned off as Lot 454. "I stole the idea from her," Bush frankly admitted.

Lots 1148 and 1149 "A French Provincial Style Painted Chest of Drawers" and "A Chippendale Style White-Painted Tall Chest of Drawers": These were actually Caroline Kennedy's and were part of her bedroom furnishings in the White House but in the catalog, there is a 1961 photo of Caroline sitting in her bedroom holding her infant brother John in her lap as President Kennedy tickles John and nanny Maud Shaw looks on. The two pieces of furniture are visible in the photo. The French Provincial Chest of Drawers was valued at between $500 and $700 and the Chippendale piece, between $600 and $800. The French Provincial piece sold for **$23,000**; the Chippendale, for **$13,800.**

Lot 1160 A gelatin silver print of Caroline's childhood White House cat Tom Kitten. The print is mounted and signed by the artist Joseph R. Spies. Tom Kitten (aka Tom Terrific) was technically Caroline's but as we all know, a household pet is usually a family pet and so, this artifact of John and Caroline's White House childhood is also associated with John Jr. It was valued at between $50 and $75. The print sold for **$14,950**.

Lot 1178 "A Study Of Caroline And John Kennedy": This is a lovely charcoal and chalk sketch of Caroline and John by Aaron Shikler done on blue paper. A barefoot eight-year-old John is shown lying on his back with a book propped on his stomach, and ten-year-old Caroline is seated next to him either writing or drawing in a book. This signed and dated piece measured 10 x 12 1/2 inches and was valued at between $2,000 and $3,000. It ultimately sold for **$54,625**.

Lot 1179 "John F. Kennedy, Jr. Seated": A colored crayon and pastel sketch on paper by Aaron Shikler that measures 9 1/4 x 6 1/2 inches and was valued at between $2,000 and $3,000. It shows John seated with his legs drawn towards his chest and his arms clasped on his knees. This was also signed and dated by the artist. The sketch sold for **$27,600**.

Lot 1181 "John F. Kennedy, Jr. Reading": This is a 1968 oil painting of the study of John in Lot 1178. It measured 6 x 10 inches, was signed by Aaron Shikler, and was valued at between $3,500 and $5,000. It is an impeccable rendering of John painted in blue and gray tones. The painting sold for **$34,500**.

Lot 1182 "A Portrait Study of John F. Kennedy, Jr.": This 7 x 9 3/4" oil painting by Aaron Shikler shows two views of John Jr. from the shoulders up. It is done primarily in orange and beige tones and was valued at between $1,500 and $2,000. It was signed and dated by Shikler. The painting ultimately sold for **$24,150**.

Lot 1192 "Photograph of an Aaron Shikler Portrait": This was a 4 x 6 inch black and white photograph of Lot 1182 and was valued at between $50 and $75. The photograph sold for **$7,187**.

All told, auction items pertaining to John Jr. sold for a whopping **$530,812**.

Preliminary proceeds and distributions for the first $30 million taken in from the auction were announced in early May (before the final figures were calculated). The take was split up as follows:

Total proceeds to the Kennedy estate: $27 million
Gross inheritance to John and Caroline Kennedy: $16.3 million
Net inheritance to John and Caroline Kennedy: $3.85 million each
Federal inheritance tax on John and Caroline's share: $8.6 million
Federal income tax on Kennedy estate: $10.7 million
Sotheby's 10 percent commission: $3 million

Corporate tax on Sotheby's commission: $1 million
Total increase in federal revenues: $20.3 million

The *Seinfeld* episode, "The Bottle Deposit"   In this 1996 episode, Elaine is given the task of bidding for J.F.K.'s golf clubs at the Sotheby auction for her boss, Mr. Peterman. He authorizes her to spend up to ten thousand dollars and Elaine drafts Jerry to go with her to the auction.

When they arrive, they bump into Sue Ann, the "Braless O Henry Candy Heiress" (don't ask!) who immediately starts throwing zingers at Elaine, implying that she is completely out of her element at such a tony (and expensive) affair. Caught up in the competitive atmosphere Sue Ann initiated by bidding against her, Elaine ends up bidding twenty thousand dollars for the clubs—spending double what her boss authorized.

The clubs end up bent and ruined when a psychotic mechanic throws them out of Jerry's car as Kramer and Newman pursue him in a mail truck.

(Incidentally, the fourth season *Seinfeld* episode "The Opera" had a "Kennedy assassination conspiracy" theme. In this installment, Jerry debunks Kramer and Newman's "Magic Loogie" theory with a slow-motion demonstration proving it was impossible for one spit loogie to have hit as many people as Newman and Kramer claimed. There must have been, Jerry concludes, a "second spitter.")

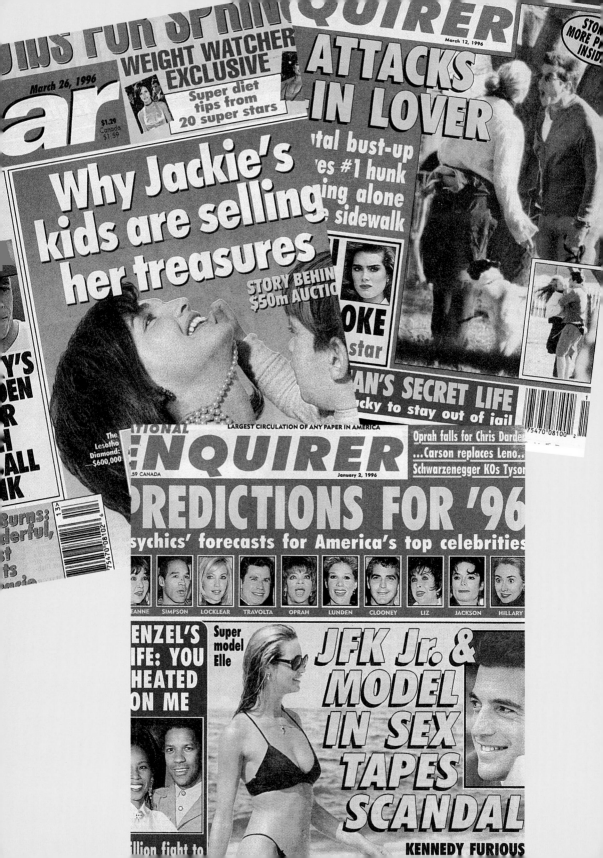

7

TABLOID TALK: SIX EXAMPLES OF HOW A FEW SUPERMARKET RAGS "COVERED" J.F.K. JR. IN 1996

The supermarket tabloids love J.F.K. Jr., and stop at nothing to run a story—*any* story—about him. Here is a look at a handful of articles about our favorite editor and Rollerblader.

The *National Enquirer*, January 2, 1996

Cover Headline   JFK Jr. & MODEL IN SEX TAPES SCANDAL: KENNEDY FURIOUS but Elle MacPherson laughs!

Cover Photos   Elle MacPherson on a beach in a black bikini; plus an inset head shot of John smiling.

Story   This story, headlined "JFK Jr. Caught in Steamy Sex Tapes Scandal," begins, "John Kennedy Jr. is reeling from a steamy sex-tape scandal!" The *Enquirer* reports on a story originally from the British tabloid the *Sunday Mirror* alleging that a former Beverly Hills Hotel receptionist was trying to sell tapes of voice-mail messages that John supposedly left for Elle MacPherson when the supermodel was staying at the hotel. The *Mirror* headlined their story, "What J.F.K. Jr. told supermodel Elle in sexy hotel messages: I wanna do it with you." The *Mirror* alleges that John left messages for Elle that said, "You are the fantasy I long to fulfill," "You have such nice buns," "Let me show you how we can have a wonderful time together," and "What I fantasize about doing to you I can only reveal when we're alone together." The story claims that John became "obsessed" with the supermodel after seeing her naked in a *Playboy* spread. The story quotes an unnamed "close friend" of John's, an unnamed "source close to Carolyn [Bessette, John's girlfriend]", and an additional unnamed "another source." The *Enquirer* also quotes John (via the aforementioned "close friend") as saying, "When I find the people responsible for this I'm going to strangle them with my bare hands!" The story also alleges that John's girlfriend Carolyn Bessette was still upset with John for having a fling with Cindy Crawford during the time they worked together shooting the first cover of his new magazine *George.*

A sampling of some of the unwanted attention John has received from the tabloids over the past few years.

Official Comment   John's personal assistant RoseMarie Terenzio told The *Enquirer*, "There is absolutely no truth to this story. Mr. Kennedy has not called Elle MacPherson and left any messages." Elle MacPherson's manager said that Elle's only reaction to the story was "to laugh at it," and that "[Elle] has a boyfriend, Tim Jeffries. He's not angry. I'm sure he feels the same way we do."

(See Chapter 6, "Scandals," for details on the March 12, 1996 *National Enquirer* issue that featured the cover story, "JFK ATTACKS LIVE-IN LOVER.")

The *National Enquirer*, March 19, 1996

Cover Headline   "Lowdown on GIRLFRIEND WHO DROVE JFK TO TEARS"

Cover Photo   A photo of Carolyn Bessette shouting at John.

Story   Basically, this story (a follow-up to the previous week's spread about their argument in the park, referred to on page 97) provided some widely-known background information about Bessette, padded with some anonymous comments from "pals" of Carolyn as well as *New York Post* columnist Cindy Adams.

The *Star*, March 26, 1996

Cover Headline   "Why Jackie's kids are selling her treasures"

Cover Photo   The infant John tugging on his mother's three-strand fake pearl necklace; plus five photos of jewelry from the Sotheby's catalog.

Story   This hyperbolic story begins, "Anguished John F. Kennedy Jr. is wracked with guilt after agreeing to sell his mother's most prized possessions," and gets worse from there.

The piece quotes unnamed "insiders" and alleges that John was emotionally exploding at the drop of a hat due to the stress attached to organizing the Sotheby's auction of his mother's things.

According to the *Star*, John and Caroline were ambivalent about selling off their parents' treasures to the highest bidders, but they had no qualms at all about getting rid of stuff Jackie had received from Aristotle Onassis. The *Star* alleges that John never liked Ari and felt no remorse about selling off anything having to do with him. This is blatantly untrue since countless other sources have acknowledged that John was quite fond of Onassis and greatly enjoyed their times together.

The remainder of the article detailed the estimated values of several of the jewelry items in the Sotheby's catalog.

Official Comment   None.

The *National Examiner*, April 2, 1996

Cover Headline "JFK JR'S SECRET DOUBLE LIFE! Why a woman just might not want to date this hunk"

Cover Photo John in a bathing suit, seen from the thighs up.

Story This "exposé" comes across as a forum for Nellie Bly, author of *The Kennedy Men*, to trash John.

The piece begins, "He's drop-dead gorgeous, has a killer body and a luscious mane most gals can't wait to run their fingers through. But hold on— John F. Kennedy Jr. may not be the hunky dream man everyone thinks he is."

Bly theorizes that John has Addison's disease (the same disease his father had); he's being treated for it with the powerful steroid cortisone, and that "steroid rage" caused his argument with Carolyn in the park a few weeks earlier.

Puh-leeeze.

Bly pulls out all the stops in her trashing of John in this piece, asserting that John is not that smart; that his magazine is a disappointment; and that since he comes from "a long line of womanizers," no parent would want him as a husband for their daughter.

And people wonder why celebrities sue tabloids.

Official Comment None.

The *National Examiner*, April 23, 1996

Cover Headline "DI AND FERGIE FEUD OVER JFK JR."

Cover Photo The same photo of John in a bathing suit that was on the cover of the *Examiner*'s April 2 issue.

Story The subtitle of this story read, "Jealous princess and duchess both crave hunk's love." Again, unnamed royal "insiders" tell their tales and reveal that both royal babes want America's Prince Charming for their very own. Carolyn had better keep her eye on John the next time they visit Great Britain, wouldn't you say? Merry Olde England is apparently a hotbed of unrequited royal lust!

Official Comment None.

[See Chapter 3, "Isn't It Romantic," for details on the May 7, 1996 *National Enquirer* issue that featured the story, "Springtime in Paris with JFK Jr. and his ladylove."]

The *National Enquirer*, July 30, 1996

Cover Headline None.

Cover Photos None.

Story   On page three of this issue was a story headlined, "JFK JR. TO RUN FOR PRESIDENT." Three pictures accompanied the piece, one of John and Carolyn Bessette, one of John's grandmother Rose Kennedy, and one of John's mother, Jackie.

The story began: "John Kennedy Jr. has made a monumental decision— he will fulfill the cherished dream of his mother and grandmother and run for the Presidency!" According to the story's author, *Enquirer* Senior Reporter Jeffrey Rodack, John's plan is to run for the U.S. Senate against Al D'Amato in 1998, win, serve two years in the Senate, and then run as the Democratic Presidential nominee in the 2000 election.

Rodack claims that John has had this master plan in the works for quite some time and that his marriage to Carolyn Bessette (which the *Enquirer* alleged was inevitable) is also a part of his political strategy. Rodack quotes an unnamed "family insider" who said, "While his candidacy has not been made public yet, John has secretly agreed to run against D'Amato. And John is expected to be a sure winner."

The article also quotes *John himself* through an also-unnamed "confidante" who has John saying, "My mother always had a dream that I would be President someday and I'm going to fulfill that dream." John allegedly continued, "When I was younger I rebelled and told her, 'I'm not going to be another Kennedy politician. My father was murdered, my uncle Bobby was murdered trying to become President.' It was all too sad and has bad memories for me. But now, I realize my father and uncle saw that by being President they could help the country and the world."

This is an especially interesting story for the *Enquirer* to run the same week that the August 1996 issue of *George* appeared on the stand. This issue of *George* included a John Kennedy interview with former *Enquirer* editor Iain Calder in which John tells Calder he has read "quotes" by him in the *Enquirer* that he *never* said. [See the chapter "In His Own Words."]

Official Comment   None.

Clippings File: A Look at Some Interesting Newspaper and Gossip Column Stories About John

John F. Kennedy Jr. has been in the newspapers and gossip columns literally since before he was born and the number of mentions and items about him and his endeavors has not let up as he's matured and been christened the "Sexiest Man Alive."

Sometimes these brief items are quite revealing and entertaining and provide a glimpse into some of the things that go on his life when he's not behind closed doors. Oftentimes, they are also unbelievably catty and sarcastic and illustrate why high-profile people like John et al go out of their way to avoid the media like the plague it often is. (See the *Daily News* blurb below about John's Christmas holiday at the Phoenician Resort for a perfect example of how these blind items can get really mean-spirited.)

In no particular chronological or subject order, then, here is a look at several months of brief mentions of John (and his sister Caroline) as they appeared in the *New York Daily News*, the *New York Post*, *USA Today*, taken from the Associated Press wire, and elsewhere.

The *New York Post* "John Kennedy at the new club Embassy on Hudson and Franklin. Robert De Niro was there same time. Remember De Niro on the cover of JFK's *George*? Well, by George, they didn't even say hello."

Associated Press "Finally speaking out in his own defense, John F. Kennedy Jr. downplayed the quarrel he had with his girlfriend while paparazzi shutters whirred.

"Talking on Howard Stern's radio show, the thirty-five-year-old bachelor refused to say whether he plans to marry Calvin Klein publicist Carolyn Bessette, and he denied rumors she's pregnant.

"Kennedy blamed 'media hysteria' for blowing it out of proportion.

" '[Of] all the dumb things that you could argue about, it was some silly argument . . . but then you read about it and it turns into something much bigger.' "

USA Today "Caroline and John F. Kennedy Jr. dig deeper into the social whirlpool. They've just been announced as honorary chairs of the 25th anniversary benefit gala of Washington's Kennedy Center for the Performing Arts April 27, [1996], with the Clintons and the Gores as patrons."

Cindy Adams/The *New York Post* "And pay attention because this is like semi-almost-major. I am told JFK Jr. visited Princess Di for thirty minutes at the Carlyle last week [the week of December 11, 1995]. I am told he schlepped a portfolio showing stuff dealing with his *George* magazine. I am told John's portfolio upended in the elevator, spilling out its contents, which is how these people, whoever they are, knew. But the ultra-refined Carlyle execs won't confirm. Or deny. Or burble anything but how discreet their hotel is."

The *New York Post* "SIGHTINGS: John Kennedy at Spy Bar telling friends he wants to interview Fidel Castro—who provided Kennedy's father with his worst days (the Bay of Pigs) and his best (the Cuban missile crisis) for his *George* magazine."

The *New York Daily News* "WHAT'S IN A NAME? For John Kennedy Jr., it always comes back to George. Of all the waiters at Joe Allen's, he got—you guessed it—George. Suppose he knows there's a magazine named for him?"

The *New York Post* "*Manhattan File* magazine has launched its own 'Best-dressed List of New Yorkers 40 and Under.' . . . John Kennedy . . . [was] among those who were chosen."

The *New York Post* "The mystery woman seen lately on the arm of . . . John Kennedy [is] mysterious no longer. JFK, Jr.'s unidentified brunette, caught on camera with the Superhunk at a recent Knicks game, is none other than his dutiful office assistant, RoseMarie Terenzio."

The *New York Daily News* "Turns out John Kennedy Jr.'s color is not a nice windburn from rollerblading through Central Park. It's actually a nice tan he picked up from vacationing at the Phoenician Resort in Scottsdale, Ariz., over the Christmas holidays.

"The pricey and ultracool resort—which got major financing from savings-and-loan scoundrel Charles Keating—is known for its seven pools, five golf courses and pricey and private villas. Last week it was also known for John-John and his lady Carolyn Bessette prancing about. Our pals spotted Kennedy buying golf clubs and baseball caps to take back home. Incidentally, the resort's lack of beaches and bridges make it a logical haven for John's uncles and cousins."

The *New York Post* "The departure of editor Eric Etheridge after just two issues of *George* magazine maybe shouldn't have been such a surprise to industry observers.

"As we noted here last year, John F. Kennedy Jr. offered only two-issue contracts to the start-up staff of his politics-and-lifestyles publication.

"Etheridge and a few others apparently weren't renewed at the end of that period. Insider's at *George*'s backer, Hachette Filipacchi Magazines, insist that the majority of staffers now have longer-term contracts."

USA Today "*George* magazine has thrown its party hat into the Academy Awards-night ring. The political mag has sent out invites for 75–100 to watch the show Monday at the Washington, D.C. home of Peggy and Conrad Cafritz.

"Co-hosts are Buffy and Bill Cafritz, also top names on Washington's social scene, and *George* exec publisher Michael Berman. Yes, editor-in-chief JFK Jr. will be there, and a number of presidential hopefuls are among invitees. 'We're just putting partisan politics aside for a night to celebrate this little bit of Americana,' Berman tells us. 'We'll have an Oscar pool and see who picks better, Democrats or Republicans.' "

The *New York Post* "SIGHTINGS: John Kennedy and Carolyn Bessette having a fat Thursday, picking up lunch at Bubby's in TriBeCa. Don't work too hard, guys."

Rush and Molloy/The *New York Daily News* "Thirty-three years after his father sweated out the Cuban missile crisis, John Kennedy Jr. is said to be eager to have a friendly chat with Fidel Castro—and, maybe, get him to put on a powdered wig.

"What could be better than an interview with JFK's heir to show that the 'new Castro' wants to do business with America? Certainly, it would be a PR coup for the publishers of *George*, who enjoy confounding skeptics itching to pen a eulogy for the mag."

Neal Travis/The *New York Post* "The children of Jacqueline Kennedy Onassis loved their mother very much, but John F. Kennedy Jr. and Caroline Kennedy Schlossberg are said to resent the way she's controlling them from beyond the grave.

"The bulk of her fortune is locked up in a charitable trust, which reverts to her grandchildren in a little more than twenty years. When John and Caroline are in their mid-fifties, their children will take possession of their inheritance and become far richer than their parents are likely to be."

The *Daily News* "The line in Hollywood's political sands is being drawn. Last night [February 27, 1996], Democrats came to the Plaza to join John Kennedy and Caroline Kennedy Schlossberg in support of Sen. Ted Kennedy on his sixty-fourth birthday. The partyers included Barbra Streisand, Lauren Bacall, Christie Brinkley, Conan O'Brien, Chevy Chase, Whoopi Goldberg and David Crosby, along with Dennis Hopper and his betrothed, Victoria Duffy."

Associated Press "Let the bidding begin: The *National Enquirer* said Friday it has received offers 'in the $100,000 range' for a thirty-minute videotape of John F. Kennedy Jr. and his girlfriend in an ugly Central Park confrontation."

The *New York Post* "John Kennedy must have felt like a hamster about to be devoured by a python Monday night when he met up with Barbra Streisand at the Plaza fundraiser for his uncle, Sen. Ted Kennedy. Sources say Streisand has a major case of the hots for the superhunk. Brian Steel, the dashing Democrat challenging Rep. Jerrold Nadler for his Upper West Side seat, escorted Babs around the ballroom, and later enjoyed a cigar with JFK Jr. at Au Bar, where Wilhelmina was hosting a party for many women with long legs and short resumes."

The *New York Daily News* "That's no mystery blond John Kennedy Jr. has been seen around with Lately. It's the *George* magazine publisher's steady galpal Carolyn Bessette—with highlights in her hair. The two lingered for more than two hours at a romantic dinner at the 21 Club Thursday night."

Rush and Molloy/The *New York Daily News* "John Kennedy Jr. may now have to deal with rumors that he and girlfriend Carolyn Bessette are expecting a child. The couple's Sunday stroll erupted into an ugly public argument—complete with grappling and tears. . . .

"A source told the *Daily News* Friday that Bessette has told friends she is pregnant.

"Inside sources at Calvin Klein, where Bessette works as a publicist, said it was a buzz around the office that the twenty-eight-year-old was in the family way.

"Others deny it. 'It's absolutely untrue. It's ridiculous, absurd,' said Michael Berman, who publishes *George* magazine with Kennedy. 'She's not pregnant. I've spent the last three days with them and I would know.'

"Bessette was not at her office Friday."

The *New York Post* "While John F. Kennedy Jr. regularly changes both his occupation and his girlfriend, he remains consistently in vogue. The hunk is one of only three survivors on Beau Brummel's new list of America's 10 most fashionable men.

The trendy SoHo outfitter last polled its customers in 1990. This year Kennedy, Michael Douglas and Kevin Costner again made the cut, while people like Pat Riley, Tom Selleck, Jack Nicholson and Don Johnson were fashion cast-offs."

The *New York Daily News* "John F. Kennedy Jr. is apparently hoping Demi Moore can do as much for his *George* magazine as she did for *Vanity Fair* four years ago—when she posed for her famous, painted–nude shot.

"John-John could use a shot in the arm about now: His magazine has slimmed down considerably since it first hit the stands. And then there's his personal image to worry about, sullied a bit by his videotaped spat with gal pal Carolyn Bessette. Junior is reportedly hoping to come back big with a topless Demi shot for the cover of his next issue.

"The 'Mr. Showbiz' Internet entertainment site reports Mrs. Willis will pose as Martha Washington. According to the cyber 'zine, she'll don a hoop skirt and her bare breasts will be painted in a stars-and-stripes pattern. A *George* spokesman insisted that he didn't know who will be on the cover."

The *New York Post*/Business "By George! JFK Jr. thinks she's got it: John F. Kennedy Jr. has a new editor at his magazine, *George*—she's twenty-six-year-old Elizabeth Mitchell."

The *New York Post* "Has John F. Kennedy Jr. been summoned to the Paris offices of Hachette Filipacchi for a big powwow on how to sharpen and tighten up his *George* magazine? That's what we hear.

JFK ATTACKS LIVE-IN LOVER

Brutal bust-up leaves #1 hunk

JFK Jr. AND LOVER IN BRUTAL BUST-UP

He wrenches ring from her hand & ends up sobbing in the street

In an astonishing in-your-face public fight, John F. Kennedy Jr. and his live-in love screamed, pushed and shoved each other as they fought over her engagement ring and their dog.

Their incredible battle royal left the precious ring broken into pieces.

The scrap began in a New York City park and spilled over into the city sidewalks — reaching a bizarre climax when macho 35-year-old JFK Jr. sat openly weeping on a street corner.

The astonishing drama erupted without warning as the hunk and blonde fiancee Carolyn Bessette, 29, took a Sunday morning stroll. The eye-popping action was captured in an amazing sequence of exclusive ENQUIRER pictures.

"At one point furious Carolyn leaped at John and grabbed him around the neck — I thought she was going to strangle him on the spot," said a stunned observer.

By DAVID WRIGHT and PATRICIA TOWLE

John, publisher of "George" magazine, and Carolyn, a public relations executive for Calvin Klein, have lived together since last spring. As The ENQUIRER revealed in September, John bought his sweetheart an engagement ring after she threatened to dump him over his summer fling with movie sexpot Sharon Stone.

John and Carolyn both seemed in a good mood on the morning of their big ruckus, Feb. 25. They began by having breakfast in a coffee shop near their Greenwich Village apartment with Carolyn bundled in heavy clothes to protect against the cold.

But by the time John and Carolyn reached the park, taking along their black and white dog Friday on a leash, they were snarling at each other. An ugly scene soon ensued, said an eyewitness.

"Suddenly they were in each other's faces, shouting angrily. They started pushing and shoving, and Carolyn yelled: 'What's your problem?' Calm down!'

"Then John shocked Carolyn by going on the attack. He violently slammed his left hand down on her wrist and ripped her diamond ring right off her finger. She shook her hand as if he'd hurt her finger and begins crying quietly.

"She accused him of breaking the ring as he pulled it off. The stone had come apart from the band.

"But John was still in a rage. His right hand shot out and grabbed her hand that had the ring and..."

(Continued on Page 35)

THE GLOVES ARE OFF! Tempers flare as JFK Jr. and his blonde girlfriend Carolyn Bessette square off face-to-face in a screaming match.

AN IRATE Carolyn gestures in disgust as hunky John tries to take off at the height of the incredible battle.

BOILING POINT: John is bursting with rage.

A DISTRAUGHT John (left) sits crying on the sidewalk until Carolyn approaches (above) and kneels down as if to console him. Finally, (right) the two enemies become lovers again.

ENQUIRER PHOTO EXCLUSIVE

"Late in the day, young JFK's p.r. machine found out about the above item. They say everything's ducky at *George*, with no fix-up trips to Paris planned. Okay, denial duly noted."

The *New York Post* "Who is the mystery couple willing to ante up $4 million to $6 million for a new Central Park Children's Zoo? Some followers of the controversy over what to do about the obsolete facility are convinced that it's Caroline Kennedy and Edwin Schlossberg. 'It just makes sense,' says one close to the action. 'The amount is close to what Caroline and John Kennedy expect to raise in the auction of [Jackie Kennedy's things]. Not to mention that the Parks Department has been trying to squeeze money out of them for a while. They renamed the reservoir for Jackie Kennedy Onassis in the hope that Caroline and John would donate money to the park, but so far, that hasn't happened. Maybe they've finally got them with the children's zoo.' Or maybe not. A spokeswoman for Schlossberg flatly denies he and his wife are the benefactors: 'It's not them.' "

The *New York Post* "It's a busy week for Kennedy clan watchers in New York.

"On one front, John Kennedy's combative companion is quitting her post with Calvin Klein and John-John himself is trading in his Rollerblades for a muscle car. . . .

"Regarding the career-climbing of John's girlfriend Carolyn Bessette, sources say she's finally jumping the designer's fashionable ship after seven years in public relations and moving on to points unknown. . . .

"Our spy in Bedminster Township, N.J. says JFK rode into a local auto refurbishing outfit on his bicycle—unrecognized by the dealers at first—and inquired about vintage ragtops.

"His first choice was a Volkswagen Carmen Ghia convertible, but he couldn't find one that wasn't too rotten to refurbish. After deciding on a GTO, he looked at six and chose one that will cost $20,000 by the time it's restored.

"After agreeing on the price, the dealer offered to throw his bike in the back of a truck and give Kennedy a ride home—presumably to Jackie's former summer home on 10 acres in nearby Bernardsville.

"Replied JFK, 'Thanks, but my sister can pick me up if I need a ride.' Kennedy's rep didn't call us back."

The New York Post   "WE HEAR . . . that Jackie O's three-hundred-acre estate on Martha's Vineyard has been sold for just $2 by the trust which held it for the former First Lady. The buyers, who each paid $1? Caroline Kennedy Schlossberg and John Kennedy."

The New York Post   "SURVEILLANCE: John Kennedy telling sister Caroline at San Domenico how he's going to get more personal in his editor's note in *George*."

The New York Post   "Details are still under wraps and in development, but we've learned that John Kennedy Jr.'s *George* magazine is revving up to reinvent itself via America Online with a soon-to-debut site, featuring original material not included in the monthly glossy. Word has it that writers are currently being hired for the mag's new spinoff with bestselling author John Calvin Batchelor being one of the first to sign on for a regular rightwing-slinging column tentatively titled 'CYBERGOP.'"

The New York Post   "[D]o you recall that we recently ran an item reporting that young John had been called to Paris to confer with Hachette Filipacchi execs over the direction of his *George* magazine? I do find it interesting that we received a rebuke from his press reps. John was *not* in Paris, said they, and had no plans to go to Paris, Despite those disclaimers, he popped up there a week ago with his girlfriend Carolyn Bessette.

"Plans change, I guess—just like magazine mastheads."

The *New York Post*   "SIGHTINGS: John Kennedy and his woman, Carolyn Bessette, on the Boston-N.Y. shuttle last Thursday [May 30, 1996] going over what seemed to be a seating chart for a (engagement?) party."

The *New York Post*   "Don't invite the great artist Aaron Shikler and the offspring of Jacqueline Kennedy Onassis, John and Caroline, to your next high tea.

"Shikler, whose official portraits of Jackie and JFK hang in the White House, is more than a little annoyed that the Kennedy kids included his sixteen or seventeen sketches of their mother in the famous Sotheby's auction. The sketches sold for large sums, and even photos of the sketches went for big bucks.

"Shikler felt his renderings of the former First Lady weren't in the 'for sale' class and should have been offered instead as a legacy to family and friends."

The *New York Post*   "SIGHTINGS: John Kennedy and Carolyn Bessette yesterday [July 22, 1996] on the 7:35 A.M. flight from Martha's Vineyard, where they presumably weekended at the huge estate his mother left him and Caroline."

The *New York Daily News*/"Hot Copy"   "JFK Jr. takes the cake: The guys who run *George* magazine made a great score when they got Barbra Streisand to pose for an upcoming cover, one that features the most compelling women in politics today. But they apparently went too far with their initial plans for the way the diva was to appear.

"See, John Kennedy Jr. and his staff originally wanted Babs to dress like Marilyn Monroe and pose with a birthday cake—since this is the year our President Clinton turns 50. Suffice it to say, Babs nixed the idea of becoming the Cake Lady.

"Instead, our source said, she opted to dress like Betsy Ross . . . because she reportedly felt the Marilyn look would hurt the President and give the impression of his being a philanderer.

"Nice try, though, guys."

***USA Today*/Jeannie Williams**   "On the brink of marriage? *W* predicts JFK Jr. and Bessette will wed soon: Wedding bells could toll soon for John F. Kennedy Jr. and Carolyn Bessette, according to the August *W* magazine. It keeps a close eye on the fashion world, where Bessette was a star with Calvin Klein's operation.

"*W*'s theory is that Bessette, twenty-nine, quit Klein, where she was a publicist, to craft an image as the perfect Kennedy wife. 'No more wild friends. No more male models. No more late nights. She moved into [Kennedy's] TriBeCa loft and is working hard to be the quintessential helpmate,' *W* suggests.

" 'She's got Princess Di and Jackie O down pat,' [says a former colleague]. 'She does the wave. She knows how to get out of a limousine. But she's modernized it. It's Street Chic.' "

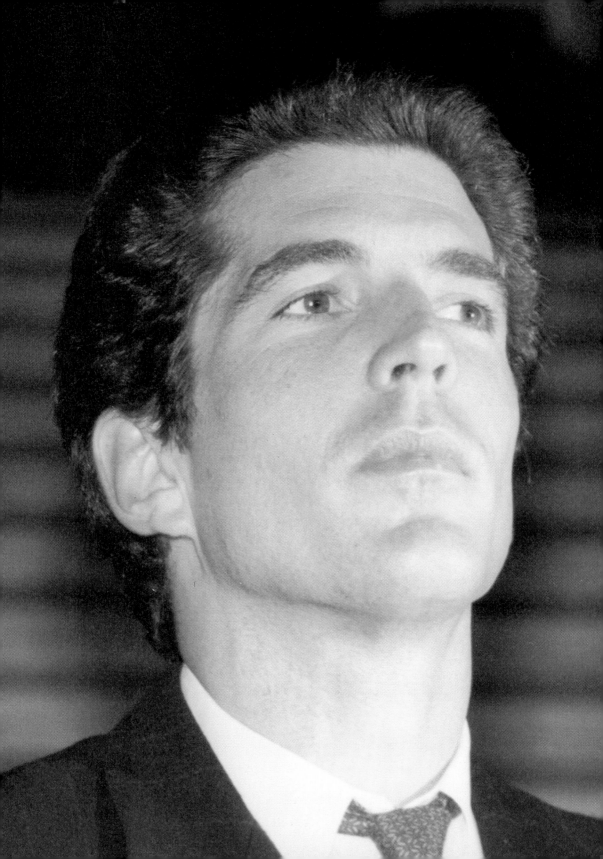

8

IN HIS OWN WORDS: J.F.K. JR. SPEAKS

It isn't often that John Kennedy Jr. speaks to the media, and when he does, it is usually a very structured situation with limits on both time and topics.

Thus, it is hard to know the real John. He is not forthcoming about his personal life, nor does he divulge his personal opinions on political, economic, or social issues.

This section collects a sampling of quotations from John made over the past decade or so and will hopefully serve as the next best thing to a personal interview with America's most fascinating Kennedy.

On J.F.K.'s legacy:

I think [Caroline and I] have a strong sense of my father's legacy and how important it is and we both respect it enormously. But at the same time, there is a sense of—a realization that things are different and that he would have wanted us to go on our own lives and not re-enact his. . . . You have to remember that both my sister and I, particularly myself, view my father's administration through the color of others and the perceptions of others and through photographs and through what we have read. And so it's difficult for us to discern much about him independently of what other people's impressions are. (From an interview with Jay Schadler on ABC-TV's "*Prime Time Live*," May 21, 1992.)

On Oliver Stone's movie *JFK*:

Shortly after Oliver Stone's controversial movie *JFK* was released, the media began hounding John about it. And the most asked question was, of course, "Have you seen the movie?" At that time, John was quoted as saying, "I haven't seen the film and I don't intend to. How I feel about my father's death is a personal, family matter." However, in a 1995 interview with Warren Beatty for the second issue of his magazine *George*, the following exchange took place:

John at his most regal, wouldn't you say? PHOTO: PHOTOFEST

JOHN F. KENNEDY JR.: The real question is: Can people learn American history through film? For example, the year that *JFK* came out, everyone suddenly had an opinion on the circumstances surrounding my father's death. Now this Christmas, because of Stone's new movie, there will probably be millions of Nixon experts.

WARREN BEATTY: I can't resist asking whether you saw *JFK*.

JOHN F. KENNEDY JR.: I didn't. Though I probably should have.

WARREN BEATTY: Why didn't you?

JOHN F. KENNEDY JR.: I didn't want to. But the ideas in the film became fixed in the public psyche—for a year it seemed that was all anyone talked about—Jim Garrison, Johnson, my father, the CIA. In an odd way, it wasn't that different from the first hundred days of this Congress, when everyone was talking about the Contract With America— that ability of politics and film to get lots of people talking about the same thing.

In December 1991, *Time* magazine reported that John was extremely upset with the then-new Oliver Stone film *JFK* and was also quite distressed that the painful subject of his father's assassination was now a hot topic for discussion throughout the country and around the world. They quoted John as dejectedly saying, "Maybe I'll just have to leave town."

On his memories of his father:

JOHN F. KENNEDY JR.: I have a few. He had this desk in the Oval Office which was made—which belonged to a sea captain. And the—it was made from an American frigate. And I just remember the inside that you could climb around in, and there were kind of cavernous spaces in it and we used to. . . .

JAY SCHADLER: You remember crawling inside?

JOHN F. KENNEDY JR.: Yeah, and just hanging out there. And he used to give us chewing gum because my mother didn't like us to chew gum, so we used to go over to the Oval Office at night and he'd feed us gum under the desk. (*PrimeTime Live*)

On whether or not he'll ever enter politics:

If your father was a doctor, and your uncle are doctors, and all your cousins are doctors, and all the family ever talks about is medicine, there's a good chance maybe you're going to be a doctor too. But maybe you want to be a baker. (Quoted in *People*, August 16, 1993)

It takes a certain toll on your personality and on your family life . . . So if I were to do it, I would want to make sure that it was what I wanted to do and that I didn't do it because people thought I should. (Quoted in *Ladies Home Journal*, September 1995)

I hope eventually to end up as president . . . of a very successful publishing venture. (At the press conference announcing the debut of his magazine *George*)

[M]y father was in politics. My uncles were in politics. My cousins are in politics. We grew up amidst political life . . . but the answer is a big "I don't know yet." (*Prime Time Live*)

I don't rule out anything. Public service should be something that you bring yourself wholly to and . . . I have sort of a life to live before I want to think about that. (To Barbara Walters on her special *The Ten Most Fascinating People of 1995*)

I have to admit, it is something I consider a lot. Once you run for office, though, you're in it. Sort of like going into the military—you'd better be damn sure that it is what you want to do, and the rest of your life is set up to accommodate that. (Quoted in the January 1995 issue of *Good Housekeeping* magazine)

On what he would do if he were elected President of the United States:
I think I would have to call my uncle Teddy and gloat for a moment and then . . . I think I would probably offer a big tax cut before the next election and hopefully in between try to do some good. (To Barbara Walters)

On tabloid journalism:
What about the personal lives of politicians? What can they do to avoid the scrutiny: "Have you ever done drugs?" "Have you ever committed adultery?" Is all that really anybody's damned business? (From John's interview with former *Enquirer* editor Iain Calder in the August 1996 issue of *George*)

On being perceived as a sex symbol:
Listen, people can say a lot worse things about you . . .than you are attractive and you look good in a bathing suit. (To Barbara Walters)

On how he felt when he showed up for his first day of work at the New York District Attorney's office and found hordes of media awaiting his arrival:
More relaxed until I saw you guys. (To the gathered media)

On the most intriguing thing about his father:
I think the most interesting thing about him is that you realize that he was just a man, that he lived a life, like anybody else. (From an ABC interview)

On planning his mother's funeral:
> In choosing the readings, we struggled to find one that captured my mother's essence. Three attributes came to mind over and over. They were the love of words, the bonds of home and family, and her spirit of adventure.

On how he felt about acting in 1981 after appearing in Shakespeare's *The Tempest*:
> I don't plan to make acting my profession—although I do enjoy it.

On his six-performance professional acting debut in 1985 in *Winners*, by Brian Friel:
> This is definitely not a professional acting debut by any means. It's just a hobby.

On how he felt after failing the New York State Bar exam the first time:
> I have to give it everything I've got next time so I don't go through this again.

On how he felt after failing the New York State Bar the second time:
> I'm very disappointed. But you know, God willing, I'll go back there in July and I'll pass it then. Or I'll pass it the next time, or I'll pass it when I'm ninety-five. I'm clearly not a major legal genius. I hope the next time you guys are here will be a happy day. (To the swarming media)

On how he felt after finally passing the New York State Bar exam:
> I'm very relieved. It tastes very sweet at the moment. (To the ever-present media)

John's tongue-in-cheek answers to "the most frequently asked personal questions":
> Yes; no; we're merely good friends; none of your business; honest, she's my cousin from Rhode Island; I've worn both; maybe someday, but not in New Jersey. (Said at the press conference announcing the publication of *George*)

On why he attended the William Kennedy Smith rape trial:
> He's helped me out in the past and I was glad to come and be of assistance. Willie is my cousin. We grew up together. I thought I could at least be with him during this difficult time. (To the gathered press)

On why he got into publishing:
> I think the idea was somewhat inevitable. Both my parents not only loved words but spent a good part of at least their professional lives in the word business. (*Esquire*, September 1995)

On why he decided to create a political magazine:
My mother knew something about politics. It was said she was the only person in the Administration who could get along with DeGaulle. And my father knew something about journalism. Fifty years ago he was a working reporter covering the United Nations in San Francisco. For me, the marriage of publishing and politics simply weaves together the two family businesses. (At the *George* press conference)

On what his mother might think of his new career as a publisher:
My mother would be mildly amused to see me up here, and very proud. (At the *George* press conference)

What his family thinks of *George*:
Uncle Ted said, "John, if I'm still talking to you by Thanksgiving, you're not doing your job."

On his preparation for launching *George*:
Three days. I took this seminar for magazine start-ups. The guy said there are some subjects that lend themselves to successful magazines because they have natural advertising support, and some subjects that don't. He said the two that come to mind that don't are religion and politics. (At the *George* press conference)

On the meaning of politics and his perception of it in the big picture:
One of our premises [with *George*] is that politics and culture are not two separate worlds sealed off from one another, but each helps shape the other. I was a little young in 1960 to notice the sea change then, but in my own life, I think 1992 was a similar benchmark in our understanding the opportunities that were created by this new way of covering politics.

His thoughts (at the age of five) after hearing his Uncle Bobby tell him about windowless rat-infested Harlem apartments:
I'm going to work and I'm going to take all the money I earn and buy windows for all those houses. (From *George*)

John's campaigning "style":
Hi, I'm John Kennedy. It would be great if you would vote for my cousin. (During Patrick Kennedy's 1988 run for the Rhode Island state legislature.)

On the mingling of politics and entertainment:
Politicians have taken their cue from the entertainment industry. Al Gore on David Letterman was that show's number-one rated show for that year. ("Al Gore," *Esquire*, September 1995)

On his mother's perception of what it meant to be in the Kennedy family:

Not being a Kennedy, my mother could recognize both the perils and the positive aspects.

On gun control and violence in America:

As a lifelong urban dweller, former prosecutor and one personally affected by gun-related violence, I've always believed that the easy availability of handguns has a great deal to do with America's distinction as the world's most violent industrialized nation. (From the introduction to John's interview with NRA president Marion Hammer in the April/May 1996 issue of *George.*)

On his speech at the 1988 Democratic convention:

There have been many memorable speeches made at national political conventions. Mine wasn't one of them. (From the "Editor's Letter" in the August 1996 issue of *George*)

On whether or not the *National Enquirer* makes up quotes:

I've read quotes in the *Enquirer* attributed to me that I've never said in my life. (From John's interview with former *Enquirer* editor Iain Calder in the August 1996 issue of *George*)

On *George* going from bimonthly to monthly publication:

This issue will, for the first time in the magazine's short history, be followed by another a month later, another a month after that, and so on. We never thought we'd get here so fast. So to all of you who have helped us and stayed with us—thank you. (From the "Editor's Letter" in the August 1996 issue of *George*)

On putting Drew Barrymore dressed as Marilyn Monroe on the September 1996 issue of *George:*

It's reprising [a song] sung to my father in 1962. I don't see what possible taste questions could be involved. If I don't find it tasteless, I don't know why anyone would. [That song] is part of the iconography of American politics. [It's] an enduring image. The magazine has played with political icons from the name on. I wouldn't be doing my job if I didn't try to come up with interesting, engaging ideas. (To *USA Today*)

On whether or not he consulted with his family before he put "Marilyn" on the cover of his magazine:

Some of them are on the comp list. They'll probably get it soon. (To *USA Today*)

On how he feels about the rumors about Marilyn Monroe and his father:

Just because people have clucked for decades, why does this make it strange we would use that bit of iconography? I'm intrigued that people would be indignant if I'm not. (To *USA Today*)

On the nickname that refuses to go away:

No one I know calls me John-John. (From a September 1996 interview with John on America Online.)

In his grandfather's day, money was power.

In his father's day, politics was power.

In his own day, media is power.

—**MICHAEL GROSS, from "Citizen Kennedy," a profile of John in *Esquire.***

John and Caroline Kennedy's childhood nanny Maud Shaw once said about the two Kennedy children:

They both have their father's gift of asking just the right questions and pursuing their interrogations until they have the right answers to satisfy them.

Her observation is borne out by John's monthly interviews in *George*. His first five interviewees were controversial former Alabama governor George Wallace, Warren Beatty, basketball star Charles Barkley, Marion Hammer (the National Rifle Association's first female president), and New Jersey governor Christine Todd Whitman. His questioning of each was insightful, smart, and sensitive.

Here is a detailed look at the first five issues of *George*, the magazine that has a President's name on the cover, and the name of a President's son on its masthead.

These five are the magazine's only bimonthly issues. In August 1996, *George* went to monthly publication, five months ahead of its projected date of December 1996. Total page count and advertising pages were down from the first couple of issues but no one at *George* believed they would be able to maintain the half a million copy sales results of the first issue anyway. Overall, it seemed as though *George* was a success and would be able to continue on, but on a smaller scale. (One source said that *George*'s backers ultimately hoped to match the *New Republic*'s monthly sales of between 100,000 and 125,000 copies.)

John answers questions about *George*. PHOTO: PHOTOFEST

On Monday, October 21, 1996, Villard Books announced a joint publishing venture with *George* magazine to do a number of books with political and cultural themes. The first two titles announced were *George's Book of Political Lists* and *George's Thousand Ideas To Help America*. It was not revealed who would be writing the books or when the books would be released, but all of the Villard "George" titles would be licensed under the aegis of *George* magazine and use the name of the magazine in the books' titles.

GEORGE: THE FIRST FIVE ISSUES

Issue Number One; October/November 1995 280 pages

Cover *Cindy Crawford dressed as George Washington.* The ever-fetching Ms. Crawford wore a soldier's uniform from the Revolutionary War era that boasted a few, ahem, modifications, most notably a tight, ruffled satin top that just so happened to bare her flawless belly all the way up to just below her breasts. She also wore a white wig, bright red lipstick and skintight yellow pants. The cover boasted that this was the "inaugural issue" of the magazine and previewed the feature stories "John Kennedy talks to George Wallace," "President Madonna," "Dodging Bullets With the FBI's Louis Freeh," and "Caleb Carr on the Next American Revolution." The cover also highlighted features on Julia Roberts, Mark Leyner and the new divas of politics.

Written on the Spine "Inaugural Issue"

The Editor's Letter John's very first words to his "Inaugural Issue" readers were:

> *"If, as some historians suggest, Americans renew their passion for politics every thirty years, perhaps this reawakening is due less to changes of heart than to changes in how the elected communicate with the electorate."*

Later, in a well-written and insightful paragraph, he defines *George* (and provides a cogent defense of the need for his new publication in the first place):

> George *is a lifestyle magazine with politics at its core, illuminating the points where politics converges with business, media, entertainment, fashion, art and science. Whether it's violence in the movies or free speech on the Internet, culture drives politics. The public arena is not a hothouse sealed off from the general climate. It partakes of it, changes it, and is changed by it.*

Features The premiere issue was informative and surprisingly entertaining, notable feats when you consider the topics it tackled: *George* succeeded in making the boring less so. Politics actually seemed vibrant and interesting and the people who lived it passionate and intriguing.

Among many well done colorful graphics, the author's favorite was the U.S. map that showed how much each state got back for every tax dollar it sent to Washington—The author was dismayed to read that his home state of Connecticut only gets 69 cents returned to it for every buck it pays out.

Some of the feature articles were terrific (although many of them could have easily appeared in forums such as *Vanity Fair* or *GQ* and fit quite nicely), especially Al Franken's solution to the budget problem (shoot senior citizens into space); the article about Julia Roberts' humanitarian trip to Haiti; the piece explaining how video polling works; and Paul Begala's astute dissection of the press.

There were also features on campaign advisers, FarmAid and Comic Relief, Candace Gingrich, and DeLores Tucker, a black liberal woman activist's war against Time-Warner and gangsta rap. Novelist Caleb Carr also contributed a lengthy (and important) think piece ("The Next American Revolution Is Now") that amplified John Kennedy's defining principle for the magazine. It was an essay that asserted that politics has entered a new age, and that this rebirth of the second oldest profession amounted to a revolution in the way the American people perceived both the political process and the people involved in it.

The premiere issue also featured book and music reviews, and it closed with Madonna's essay, "If I Were President." The Madonna piece showed that *George* had a sense of humor. Madonna was allowed to be as outrageous as she wanted to be and some of her Presidential directives would include sending Rush Limbaugh, Jesse Helms, and Bob Dole to hard-labor work camps; allowing Roman Polanski back into the country, while kicking Howard Stern out; and insisting that the entire armed forces come out of the closet.

Following his Editor's Letter, though, and until we got to his interview with George Wallace, John Kennedy was nowhere to be found in his magazine. And since we know so little about his ideology and personal views, his presence did not permeate the meat and bones of the magazine the way it probably should have.

John did do a superb job, however, with his George Wallace interview. It's difficult to know just how much of the actual writing of the introduction and the editing of the final text was done by John himself, but the intro was in the first person and was presented as a John Kennedy piece. The Wallace interview was spooky and disturbing, and John should be applauded for tackling someone like Wallace in the very first issue of a brand-new magazine. The piece was accompanied by stark black-and-white Herb Ritts photos that showed Wallace as a frail and gnome-like old man with dirty fingernails sitting in a wheelchair.

This interview forcefully sent the message that John F. Kennedy Jr. and his family held an important place in American history. John and George Wallace's discussion of President Kennedy was powerful reading. It illustrated with a singular drama the reality that political legends were flesh-and-blood people and not mythological creatures, that these men were fathers, sons, and brothers. John began the interview by acknowledging that Wallace and "certain members of my family" had had their differences over the years and Wallace responded and talked about John's father with ease.

This first issue was a slick and easily digestible package and the magazine mostly accomplished what it said it wanted: to be to politics what *Premiere* and *Rolling Stone* are to film and rock music, respectively. *George* seemed to be on the right track.

Professional layout and presentation aside, though, we still did not know the answer to the question, Does *George* have an *identity*? In this first issue, *George* seemed to have *several* identities, all of which strived to make politics as easy to take as any other element of pop culture. The monumental hype (aided by the media presence of the newly-public John) sold out the 500,000 copies of this issue and set the stage for what seemed like an overwhelming success.

Issue Number Two; December 1995/January 1996
280 pages

Cover   *Robert De Niro dressed as George Washington.* The white-bewigged De Niro is holding a saber on which is impaled an Ace of Spades. On the contents page, a note explained that the sword, "(courtesy of Caroline Kennedy) is one of five exact replicas of the one George Washington carried, right down to the worn spot on the ivory grip. The original sword is in the permanent collection of the Smithsonian." The cover previewed the stories "The Women of Watergate," "John Kennedy Talks Politics With Warren Beatty," "President Limbaugh," and "Jackpot '96: Setting the Odds on the Big Race."

Written on the Spine   "Jackpot '96"

The Editor's Letter   John starts off his second issue talking about a political movie, *The Candidate.* Noting that one of the final lines of that 1972 film about politics and campaigning is "What do we do now?" he admits that that question expressed his sentiments when he and his *George* colleagues had to put out a second issue so soon after the magazine's launch and debut issue. His Editor's Letter ends with a discussion of three new films that had political themes—*Nixon, The American President,* and *Casino*—and he notes that "much of politics, like the movies, is about star power."

Features   There were several interesting features in this issue; some successes, some failures. "The All-Apocalypse Cable Channel" by Bill Franzen fell flat, the candidate profile Q and A with Steve Forbes worked nicely.

The interview with abortion strategist Leslie Sebastian epitomized a good example of what *George* could (and should) do best: Put a human face on a complex social issue that has an intense political element and let the reader decide for him (or herself) where they stand.

A bomb, however, was the feature "The Body Electorate" in which *George* interviewed people with the same exact names as the major political candidates (an African-American waitress named Pat Buchanan; a retired biology professor named Bob Dole; a factory worker named Bill Clinton, etc.) and asked them if they'd vote for the candidate with their name. Contrived, trite, and trivial, it was really little more than a waste of pages. It probably sounded clever and cute during the editorial meeting. In actuality, it tanked.

Matthew Miller's "Demagoguery and Denial," on the other hand, should be reprinted by the millions and distributed to every taxpayer in the United States. In just two pages, Miller revealed and explained the chicanery, rhetoric, and outright lying politicians (from both parties) use to arrive at a Federal budget each year, and illustrated deftly and in easily understandable language, exactly why no one trusts politicians and why it's totally unlikely that we will see a balanced budget in this country ever again.

Bookending this piece was an incredibly infuriating piece called "Washington's Top Ten Perks" in which author Phil Hirschkorn cataloged the freebies and accommodations provided to politicians at taxpayer expense, including comprehensive health care and exercise facilities for pennies, free travel, and what is probably the best pension plan in the history of the world—a retirement program that escalates and compounds so lucratively that often politicians end up receiving up to twice their salaries upon retirement.

"Pop Politics" was a fun feature that fulfilled *George*'s stated mission: to explore how pop culture has infiltrated politics and how politics has become a part of pop culture. This survey analyzed the movies, music, and TV show tastes of people based on their political persuasions. We learned that *Philadelphia* was "the thinking-female Democrat's movie" and that Garth Brooks's fans are the most Republican and the most likely to vote for Bob Dole. "Pop Politics" worked, and it also informed while it entertained.

This second issue, in addition to John's exclusive interview with media recluse Warren Beatty, also included a feature on political dirty tricks; profiles of Federal Judge Alex Kozinsky, Jesse Jackson Jr., Anna Deavere Smith, David Kissinger, and Dick Armey; an article that looked at the odds on the '96 Presidential race; an engaging look at the women of Watergate; an amusing piece on car salesmen turned politicians; plus reviews of the movie *GoldenEye*, the cybermagazine *geekgirl*, and Salman Rushdie's new novel, *The Moor's Last Sigh*.

The capper to the issue was Rush Limbaugh's "If I Were President" column. What would Rush Limbaugh do if he were President? Post the Ten Commandments on the wall of the Oval Office and appoint Ross Perot U. S. Ambassador to the U. N., for starters. But Limbaugh also told us what he would *not* do, which included "Blame talk radio for my problems," "Jog," "Assign the revamping of the American health-care system to my wife," and "Allow my brother to sing in public."

Issue Number Three; February/March 1996   280 pages

Cover   *Charles Barkley in white wig, Colonial waistcoat, basketball shorts, and sneakers.*

The cover text announced "One on One: Charles Barkley Tells John Kennedy About His Next Move"; "Larry King: Reign-Maker"; as well as "Martha Stewart's Cherry Surprise"; "Washington's Most Dangerous Journalist?"; and "Pat Buchanan Unleashed."

Written on the Spine   "One on One"

Editor's Letter   John's letter this month was one page long and ranged from his talk with Charles Barkley to what George Washington might think if he were alive today at the age of 264.

Features   True to its mission statement, this month's opening feature, "We the People" highlighted the Fire and Ice Ball for breast cancer research and A Concert of Hope for addiction resources and displayed pix of Sharon Stone, Jim Carrey, Tony Bennett, Roseanne, Jamie Lee Curtis, Chevy Chase, Christie Brinkley, and Betty Ford.

"The Scoop" dished Washington gossip, including morality watchdog William Bennett's party that got so loud the police were called; and Frank Sinatra's foul-mouthed "review" of his hometown neighbors in Hoboken, New Jersey.

"The American Spectacle" feature was truly terrific this month. Developing a quite fascinating idea, *George* drafted Dr. Kanodia, a renowned plastic surgeon to reveal how he'd "spruce up" the faces of the leading Presidential candidates and then, using computer imaging, *George* showed us the before pictures *and* the results. Hilarious and revealing, this kind of irreverent—yet right on-the-money—spin on the political process made it obvious that this is the kind of material that *George* does best. Who needed the most improvement? Pat Buchanan, who easily looked twenty years younger following Dr. Kanodia's tinkering.

There was an interesting profile of descendants of George Washington, and a look at how illustrated sound bites worked to enhance political advertising. The feature on the top ten Washington buzzwords, however, while sounding like a great idea, came across as too "inside" to mean much to readers who do not live in Washington. Even those who follow politics would be hard pressed to recall when they had ever come across "Gergenize" or "triangulate" used in their proper "Washington" context. This piece was an example of what could happen if *George* were to get too cutesy and remain fixated inside the Washington Beltway. If Washingtonians really do live in their own world, oblivious to the real America, this piece, effectively illustrated that state of mind.

"Jesus in '96" was a humor piece by *Beavis and Butthead* writers Sam Johnson and Chris Marcil that examined what would happen if Christ were a political candidate.

A poll that questioned well-known pundits about the possible Republican presidential candidate was interesting; as was the piece about President Clinton's strategy for the 1996 campaign.

John's interview with Charles Barkley was superb! He asked pointed questions about racism, interracial marriage, the O. J. verdict, and Barkley's ambition to run for governor of Alabama.

An interesting piece of historical synchronicity presented itself in the article "The Devil and Arthur Miller" which was about Miller's defense of witches and the filming of his play *The Crucible*. Miller, of course, was married for a time to Marilyn Monroe, who allegedly had an affair with John's father, J.F.K. It is probably to John's credit that he didn't kill the piece for fear of bringing up something embarrassing from his family's past.

"The Truth About Ruth" was an interesting profile of journalist Ruth Shalit; the profile of Pat Buchanan revealed just how off-the-wall some of his ideas actually are ("The day I walk into the Oval Office is the day I start building a fence across our southwest border," "If I get elected, not one dime is going to Planned Parenthood!"); and Mark Leyner's unflattering piece about Larry King was funny but not much more than that.

Martha Stewart's recipe for cherry pie was a fun (if frivolous) feature. The issue concluded with the regular "If I Were President" feature by Dallas Cowboys owner Jerry Jones. (He'd sell marketing rights to America. The Pizza Hut Capitol Building was one of his suggestions.)

Overall, the February/March issue was well-written and well-conceived, continuing to fulfill its stated purpose of looking at politics, pop culture, and lifestyles, all in the same magazine.

Issue Number Four; April/May 1996   156 pages

Cover   *Howard Stern in Ben Franklin glasses and a ruffled shirt, holding a chainsaw and standing amidst a pile of chopped-to-smithereens cherry tree branches.*

The cover asked "What's So Good About Virtue?" and highlighted the celebrities (Stern, Candice Bergen, and Oliver North) whose answers to this question were inside the magazine. At the bottom right of the cover was a quote from Howard Stern: "I cannot tell a lie."

Written on the Spine   "Virtue"

Editor's Letter   John Kennedy started by asking the question, "What do virtue and politics have to do with each other?" and then explained how that month's issue would attempt to answer that question. In his brief one-page missive to his readers, John quoted John Adams, Thomas Jefferson, and, yes, even Howard Stern.

John's Letter was illustrated by a photo of ten books: *Miss America* (by Stern); *The Good Society* (John Kenneth Galbraith); *Telling the Truth* (Lynne Cheney); *A Call to Character* (Greer & Kohl, editors); *A House Divided* (Mark Gerzon); *The Book of Virtues* (William J. Bennett); *Values Matter Most* (Ben Wattenberg); *The Moral Compass* (also by Bennett); *Poor Richard's Almanacks* (Ben Franklin); and *The Children's Book of Virtues* (again, by Bennett) stacked up and bedecked with cherries. The April/May Editor's Letter (the last one without John's picture at the top of the page) perfectly set the stage for the material inside the magazine.

Features   If the April/May issue was a game of bowling, it would be a 300. If it was an archery competition, it would be a bullseye. If it was a . . . well, you get the point.

This issue was almost perfect. It was informative and extremely entertaining, and it succeeded in being everything and more *George* seemed to want to be in its first three issues.

The issue reached for an ambitious goal: Define and examine the role of virtue in culture and politics in the late twentieth century and place our current obsession with doing "the right thing" in a context relative to the motivations of our founding fathers. (We said it was ambitious, didn't we?)

The issue had the right mix of celebrities (Howard Stern, Paul Newman, Conan O'Brien, and even The Simpsons); journalists (Tom Brokaw, Diane Sawyer), and political figures (Enid Waldholtz, Evan Bayh). It also added to the mix Joe Queenan, Tabitha Soren, Tori Amos, and the late William Kunstler's protégé, Ron Kuby.

The first feature was (perhaps symbolically?—just asking!) a photo layout illustrating the incineration of the White House by laser beams. The photos were from the summer 1996 movie *Independence Day* and were captioned, "Is nothing sacred?"

The breezy front-of-the-magazine section included some interesting sidebars and brief features. The most interesting one revealed that, even though the Federal government will no longer provide marijuana to those who need it for medicinal purposes, people who received it prior to the 1992 ban were exempt from the cut-off. Thus, eight U.S. citizens still receive three hundred joints of primo weed each month, grown on America's only legal pot farm in Oxford, Mississippi, at a cost of $250,000 a year. Is this a great country or what?

Another interesting "Scoop" was a list of President Clinton's recent reading choices. These included *The Life of Andrew Jackson* by Robert Remini; *Dixie City Jam* by James Lee Burke; *The Road Ahead* by Bill Gates; *Lincoln* by David Herbert Donald; *No Ordinary Time* by Doris Kearns Goodwin; *A World Lit Only By Fire* by William Manchester; *How the Irish Saved Civilization* by Thomas Cahill; and *Bosnia: A Short History* by Noel Malcolm.

The issue continued with a photo spread on the Whitewater acreage that has been the subject of so much C-Span airtime lately; and a humor piece by Conan O'Brien, in which the late night talk show host suggests giving everyone their own talk show as a cure for our ailing democracy.

Other interesting features included profiles of maverick lawyer Ronald Kuby, MTV's Tabitha Soren, and Hillary Clinton's staff, as well as a look at the best foreign embassies, the ongoing makeover of America's money, and a survey of the favorite political films of Hollywood and Washington insiders. (Patti Davis's fave is *Mr. Smith Goes to Washington*, Hunter S. Thompson likes *Being There*.) The cover story on virtue was stimulating and surprising; and John's interview with gun advocate and NRA president Marion Hammer was brilliant.

The issue concluded with an insightful portrait of feminist and singer/songwriter Tori Amos (one of the author's personal favorites), and Tom Brokaw's "If I Were President" in which he says one of the first things he would do would be to "summon warring parties to the White House and say, 'Stop whining and work this out, here and now.'"

Overall, a home run of an issue.

Issue Number Five; June/July 1996 144 pages

Cover *Demi Moore in a curly white wig, black wide-brimmed hat, red and white sleeves and pants, and red and white body paint covering her breasts and belly.*

Demi is pulling the strings of a George Washington puppet and it appears as though the stage is situated between her legs. The Demi Moore interview was headlined with the blurb "Sex and Politics: Demi Moore on Who's Pulling the Strings." The cover also highlighted "Bob Woodward's' Big Secret," Washington's Top 10 Media Hounds," and "Why Kids Are Ruining America," and significantly, for the first time, John's interview was titled "The John Kennedy Interview."

Written on the Spine   "Sweet Seduction"

Editor's Letter   Both "The John Kennedy Interview" and this month's Editor's Letter signaled a shift in John's visibility as the editor of *George.* For the first time, the Editor's letter featured a handsome black and white photo of John at the top of the page. Perhaps the fact that the magazine was going monthly with the next issue and would need to establish a devoted readership had something to do with this new willingness on John's part to be more visible.

In this month's Letter, John talked about children and the future; and gave a general rundown of the issue's contents. (In Chapter 7 of this book, "Tabloid Talk," we cite a clipping that quotes someone who overheard John telling his sister he was going to get more personal in his Editor's Letter but it did not happen with this issue. The Letter was a basic prologue to the issue and not a personal statement of any kind.)

Features   The front section of the magazine just didn't cut it this time. Usually an entertaining potpourri of lists, articles, sidebars, and photo spreads, it was a tad dry and easily dismissible, except for the photo feature "We the People" which had some interesting shots of high-profile people, ranging from Dennis Miller and Rosie O'Donnell, to Newt Gingrich and Nancy Reagan. (There was one interesting item that revealed that Pat Buchanan had claimed Mel Gibson's support for the presidency, something that Gibson completely disavowed, even though *Braveheart*'s blue-faced warrior does agree with Buchanan on some social issues, most notably abortion.)

The next few features were about logging in Oregon, judge and author Harold Rothwax, and litigator Elaine Jones; none of which are exactly household topics. A humor piece by Jon Stewart bombed, a look at how President Clinton's speeches get written succeeded. An interesting analysis of who might be Bob Dole's running mate followed, as did a revealing look at what it's like to actually work in the White House, a "dream job" many aspire to, but few survive.

"The Top Ten Publicity Hounds" looked at Washington's media whores. A humorous parody of *Primary Colors*, the novel by Anonymous (ultimately revealed to be *Newsweek*'s Joe Klein), was less than successful; a lengthy expose on two Cuban brothers running Florida's sugar industry was comprehensive but ultimately a little boring.

Carl Hiaasen's interview with *Striptease* star Demi Moore was interesting and provocative, if a little short; Bret Easton Ellis's think piece "Why kids are ruining America" was scary, smart, and easily the best piece in this month's issue. (It had better be a wake-up call, too.)

John's interview with Christine Todd Whitman was another success. John is a very good interviewer, and he does not disappoint in this talk with the only Republican female governor in the United States. His questions were evocative and on-target and it is not farfetched to predict a book published someday called *The John F. Kennedy Jr. Interviews*, collecting all of his *George* chats (if, of course, *George* survives and John continues to do the monthly talks).

"Off the Record," Robert Sam Anson's profile of journalist Bob Woodward was a revelation that proved something that this author has been suspecting for awhile: Compassion—a virtue critical to the survival of civility—is in short supply in this waning century and Bob Woodward is an example of the quintessential compassionless being. Anson reveals that this is a guy who prints "off the record" comments, is willing to betray a lifelong friend for a story, doesn't care if people get fired for talking to him, and uses Machiavellian manipulative techniques to break through people's barriers and persuade them to reveal things they never thought they'd ever divulge. "Off the Record" is one of the best—and most important—pieces *George* has ever published, and it is the type of thing they should do more of. Comprehensive and revealing, this piece alone was worth the price of the magazine.

The remainder of this month's issue offered a couple of book reviews, looked at black rap artists, profiled Patti Smith, and concluded with a piece by animal expert Elizabeth Marshall Thomas on what their pets reveal about the candidates.

The last page was, as usual, "If I Were President," which, this month, was written by sexy Latin singing sensation Gloria Estefan. The first thing she would do, she writes, would be to extend her term to six years, with the possibility of four more years to follow. (She makes the accurate observation that the first year of a President's term is spent learning the job; the second and third, fighting opposing forces; and the last year, campaigning.) Overall, a funny, thoughtful piece.

Summing Up

John and company have created a truly unique magazine, one that hopefully will be around for a long time to come.

THE WEDDING OF THE CENTURY

The President's Son Weds

In the October 1996 issue of his magazine *George*, John began his "Editor's Letter" with the following:

> *If Americans seem cynical about politics, they seem even more skeptical about the institution of marriage when it comes to public figures.*

Later in his essay, he pointedly talked about being famous—and being married:

> *The husband (usually) gets all the attention, while the wife is expected to gaze adoringly during every photo opportunity. They have little privacy and even less time together. But in another respect, the crises and isolation of a public life create a shared burden that can bring a couple closer.*

Was John dropping veiled hints that *he* would soon be one-half of a famous, married couple? It's possible, since this issue of *George* was on the stands shortly before his September 21, 1996 wedding.

Regardless of whether or not he was talking about himself, the truth is that John Jr. and Carolyn Bessette pulled off the surprise wedding of the century—and the mainstream press didn't even have a clue. (Those tireless tabloids, the *National Enquirer* and the *Star*, however, both had reporters and photographers in the area two days prior to the ceremony, and the *Globe* followed John and Carolyn to Turkey, the first stop of their honeymoon trip.) Overall, though, John and Carolyn's planning was so careful and so discrete, *People* magazine acknowledged their cleverness by featuring them on the cover (the "John kissing Carolyn's hand" photo seen everywhere) the following week with the headline, "Well Done!" further describing their nuptials as the "perfect, private wedding."

Just about anything John does, he does with grace and panache. This "official" wedding photo so perfectly captures the moment and is so beautifully composed, one might think it was staged. But the groom's impromptu kiss of his bride's hand following the wedding service was a spontaneous expression of love. PHOTO: COPYRIGHT 1996 DENIS REGGIE

Here is a complete dossier on the Wedding of the Century:

DATE: Saturday, September 21, 1996

TIME: 7:30 P.M.

PLACE: The First African Baptist Church on Cumberland Island, Georgia, a tiny wooden chapel built in 1893 by freed slaves after the Civil War. The chapel has no electricity and only eight pews.

TYPE OF CEREMONY: Roman Catholic, double ring; 45 minutes long.

OFFICIATING CLERGY: Father Charles O'Byrne, a Jesuit deacon from John's mother Jackie's parish, the Church of St. Ignatius Loyola.

BEST MAN: John's cousin, Tony Radziwill.

MATRON OF HONOR: John's sister, Caroline Kennedy Schlossberg.

FLOWER GIRLS: Caroline Schlossberg's daughters, Rose, 8, and Tatiana, 6.

RING-BEARER: Caroline Schlossberg's son, Jack, 3½.

THE BRIDE'S GOWN: A $40,000, pearl-colored, size 6, silk crepe gown designed in Paris by Carolyn's friend, Narciso Rodriguez for Nino Cerutti.

THE BRIDE'S BOUQUET: Lillies of the valley, Jackie's favorite flower.

THE BRIDE'S HAIR COMB: Carolyn wore a hair comb that had belonged to John's mother Jackie.

THE GROOM'S CORSAGE: A blue cornflower, his father's favorite flower.

THE GROOM'S WATCH: His father's.

THE GROOM'S OUTFIT: A custom-designed lightweight single-breasted blue wool suit with white piqué vest and a pale blue silk tie. The suit was made by Carolyn's friend, fashion designer Gordon Henderson.

THE WEDDING BANDS: Yellow gold, designed by John's friend (and owner of the Greyfield Inn, site of the reception) Janet (known as Gogo) Ferguson.

CAROLINE KENNEDY SCHLOSSBERG'S EARRINGS: Caroline wore her mother Jackie's diamond earrings.

CAROLINE KENNEDY SCHLOSSBERG'S GOWN: The Matron of Honor wore a high-waisted, navy-blue crepe silk gown that had been designed especially for her by Narciso Rodriguez for Nino Cerruti.

FLOWERS FOR THE BRIDAL PARTY: The flowers were selected by Rachel "Bunny" Mellon, a close friend of John's mother, Jackie.

FLORAL DESIGN OF THE CHAPEL: The wildflowers in the church were selected and arranged by Efigenio Pinhiero, Jackie's longtime butler.

CHAPEL LIGHTING: Candles, kerosene lamps, and flashlights. "There was a soft illumination up at the front of the church," Carol Ruckdeschel, a Cumberland native who lives next door to the chapel, told *People* magazine. "At the back it was dark. It made it so much more cozy and attractive."

MUSIC: "Amazing Grace" and "Will the Circle Be Unbroken" sung by Yulee, Florida, gospel singer David R. Davis, 40.

TRANSPORTATION FOR THE WEDDING GUESTS: Pickup trucks and vans, including one army vehicle.

FUNNY MOMENTS: During the ceremony, Caroline's son Jack, upon first seeing Carolyn resplendent in her wedding gown, asked loudly, "Why is Carolyn all dressed up?" After the ceremony, as John and Carolyn stood in a light rain by a wooden fence outside the chapel, a horse walked up and begin eating Carolyn's bouquet.

NOTABLE WEDDING GUESTS: Groom's side: Caroline Kennedy Schlossberg, her husband Edwin, and their three children; William Kennedy Smith, Tony Radziwill, Robert Kennedy, Douglas Kennedy, Timothy Shriver (John's cousins); Lee Radziwill Ross (Jackie's sister); Senator Ted Kennedy and his wife Vicki; Patricia Kennedy Lawford (John's aunt); Maurice Templesman (Jackie's late-in-life companion). Bride's side: Ann Marie Freeman (Carolyn's mother), Dr. Richard Freeman (Carolyn's stepfather); Lisa and Michael Roman (Carolyn's sister and brother-in-law).

WEDDING RECEPTION: The Greyfield Inn, a thirty-room mansion built in 1902 by the Carnegie family and owned by John's friend Gogo Ferguson.

The media scrambled to find out more about the new Mrs. J.F.K. Jr. Here, in a candid pose, Carolyn finds herself as the cover story in *New York* magazine. PHOTO: *NEW YORK*

WEDDING DINNER MENU: Snapper filets, crab, shrimp, swordfish, scallops, salad, corn.

WEDDING CAKE: A three-tiered vanilla buttercream cake decorated with fresh flowers.

BRIDE AND GROOMS'S WEDDING SONG: "Forever in My Life" by Prince.

WEDDING TOASTS: One by Tony Radziwill and one by John's uncle, Ted Kennedy.

JOHN'S OFFICIAL STATEMENT ABOUT THE WEDDING: "It was important for us to be able to conduct this in a private, prayerful, and meaningful way with the people we love."

PRENUP?: Rumor has it that Carolyn, worth (according to the *Star*) $373,000 at the time of the wedding, signed an iron-clad prenuptial agreement that has a $10 million cap, with Carolyn receiving a minimum of a million a year for the first three years following a divorce. If the couple has children when and if they split, the amounts would, of course, go up.

WEDDING COST: Estimated at approximately $600,000, including $300,000 for fifty private armed security guards and related security expenses. Private jets, wedding clothes, accommodations for the guests, flowers, and the catering made up the other expenses picked up by John.

RUMORS FLYING BEFORE AND AFTER THE WEDDING:
1. That the highly publicized fight John and Carolyn had in the park in February of 1996 was about the wedding: John wanted a small ceremony; Carolyn wanted a big one. They ultimately compromised: They had a small cer-

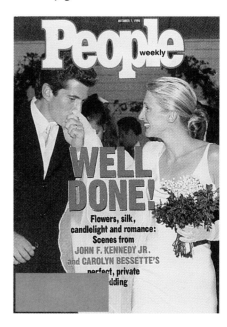

SOUVENIR SPECIAL! EXCLUSIVE WEDDING ALBUM

JFK Jr's Exotic Honeymoon

GLOBE

October 8, 1996 $1.39/$1.69 Canada

In love in Istanbul

NEWLYWEDS SLIP OFF TO TURKEY

JFK Jr.'s SECRET: BRIDE IS 9 WEEKS PREGNANT

Star

October 8, 1996 $1.39 Canada $1.69

INSIDE THEIR HONEYMOON HIDEAWAY

$10m prenuptial

Jim Carrey weds on top of mountain —and we're there

12 PAGES of great photos

CHRISTIE BRINKLEY'S 4th 'I DO' —and ex Billy Joel is there

BROOKE SHIELDS WEDS NEXT WE

JFK's WEDDING

NATIONAL **SPECIAL COLLECTORS' EDITION** **ENQUIRER**
$1.39/$1.69 CANADA   October 8, 1996

WORLD EXCLUSIVE 7-PAGE PHOTO ALBUM

Their romantic fun-filled weekend in pictures

PLUS

Meet the new Queen of Camelot

PLUS CHRISTIE BRINKLEY & JIM CARREY WEDDING ALBUMS

As you might expect, news of the secret wedding caused a media frenzy. Unaccustomed to such intense scrutiny, it must have been quite an experience for the new Mrs. Kennedy to see her wedding photo plastered everywhere.

emony for the actual wedding and they were fêted at two *gigantic* parties (one given by his sister Caroline and her husband which took place at the Schlossberg's Park Avenue apartment on Thursday, October 10, 1996, and one given by John's cousin Maria Shriver and her husband Arnold Schwarzennegger) when they returned from their honeymoon.

2. That Carolyn was nine weeks pregnant the day of the wedding. (Time will tell whether or not this rumor is true.)

3. That John changed all his phone numbers so his old girlfriends couldn't find him anymore.

4. That John and Carolyn planned on buying a place in Los Angeles, in addition to their loft in New York, and his mother's place on Martha's Vineyard.

5. That Carolyn is being groomed to be a future First Lady and that she is privately encouraging John to eventually run for president.

THE HONEYMOON: After John and Carolyn left Cumberland Island by boat, they took a sixteen-hour flight on a private jet to Istanbul, Turkey. They stayed in the Ciragan Palace ($500 a night) for three days (booked as "Mr. and Mrs. Hyannis") and then left for a tour of the Aegean Sea and the Greek Islands. John and Carolyn were discovered in Turkey by reporters and photographers for the *Globe* and John is reported to have approached them and said, "I hope you aren't going to follow us everywhere." *Globe* editor Tony Frost claimed to have called off his team after John's polite request. John and Carolyn returned to New York on Sunday, September 27, 1996. On their way out to visit friends, John and Carolyn stopped for the photographers gathered in front of their building. John asked them to be considerate of Carolyn's new public role and to understand that she is not used to the relentless media attention that he has had to deal with in his life since he was born.

It's likely that John has always known that he would not be able to wed publicly—the way his sister Caroline did in 1986. He has always gotten more attention from both the media and the American public because he has always been perceived as the only possible heir to his father's place in the White House. (And perhaps the last chance for another Kennedy to occupy the Oval Office.)

Again.

This plaintive lament seemed to echo across America and around the world the morning of Saturday, July 17, 1999.

The night before, the media announced John F. Kennedy Jr., his wife Carolyn Bessette Kennedy, and Carolyn's older sister, Lauren Bessette, were apparently missing at sea, somewhere between Long Island and Martha's Vineyard.

John, piloting his private plane, a Piper Saratoga II HP, had planned to drop off Lauren in Martha's Vineyard and then continue on to Hyannisport with Carolyn to attend the wedding of his cousin, Rory, the youngest child of Bobby Kennedy.

The three had taken off from Essex County Airport, in Fairfield, New Jersey, Friday evening, July 16, at 8:38 P.M., and had communicated with the air traffic controller there once. John was flying under Visual Flight Rules—VFR —meaning he did not have to file an official flight plan. Having received his pilot's license in May 1998, John did not yet have his pilot's instrument rating.

John flew along the Connecticut coast at 5,600 feet until 9:26 P.M., Friday evening, when, at Westerly, Rhode Island, he began his descent toward the airport on Martha's Vineyard.

At 9:40 P.M., John's plane began to plunge toward the sea at a rate of almost a mile a minute—almost ten times faster than a plane that size would normally descend. According to aviation experts, this kind of rapid descent indicated either that John's plane had experienced a major malfunction, or that John had become totally disoriented and a victim of what is known as "black hole vertigo"—an inability to distinguish up from down. John's plane hit the water with tremendous force.

After it was confirmed that John's plane was overdue, within hours a massive search-and-rescue operation began. Hoping and praying for the safety of the three, millions waited by their radios and televisions for the latest word.

Debris from John's plane soon began washing up on the shore of Martha's Vineyard. On Sunday, July 18, authorities switched their operation from

"search and rescue" to "search and recover"—confirmation that officials believed there were no survivors of the crash. All hope had vanished.

It was only after this news that the Kennedys, who had gathered at their family compound on Hyannisport, lowered their flag to half-staff. The family issued a statement that began "We are filled with unspeakable grief and sadness."

On Tuesday, July 20, the wreckage of John's plane was found on the ocean floor and within twenty-four hours the bodies of John, Carolyn, and Lauren had been recovered.

In a numbing succession of events, the bodies were transported to a local Massachusetts Medical Examiner's office, autopsied (at Senator Edward Kennedy's request, no pictures of John's body were taken), and cremated. The next morning, they were buried at sea, three miles from where John's plane had plunged into the sea.

Only immediate Kennedy and Bessette family members—including John's sister Caroline; his uncle Ted Kennedy; and cousins Maria Shriver, William Kennedy Smith, and Patrick Kennedy—were allowed on the Navy destroyer, the USS *Briscoe,* for the burial ceremony, but millions in America were there in spirit, many feeling as though they had lost a member of their own family. Memorial services—both private and public—for the three victims followed.

John was gone . . . and the world mourned the untimely death of a second John F. Kennedy.

We all came from the sea.
We are tied to the ocean.
And when we go back to the sea—
whether it is to sail or to watch it—
we are going back from whence we came.

We have salt
in our blood,
in our sweat,
in our tears.

—PRESIDENT JOHN F. KENNEDY, 1962

John was a shining light in our lives, and in the lives of the nation and the world that first came to know him as a little boy.

—From the KENNEDY FAMILY STATEMENT

I'm not sure he'd really felt that he wanted to come back to the White House before he did. But, especially in light of everything that's happened, I'm glad he had the chance to come back here one more time and see the residence and know where he was when he was a little boy. I'm glad he did that. I'm grateful that that happened.

—PRESIDENT BILL CLINTON, July 21, 1999

One sensed more about him than one knew, and what one sensed was all pretty good. He seemed to handle everything with a bouncy grace, including his share of mistakes. He didn't look or sound like a Kennedy, and did not seem to have picked up the family gene for recklessness. In short, he was as much an emblem of the family as a member of it, and for the observing public, he was useful as a figure to dream into.

—ROGER ROSENBLATT, *Time*, July 26, 1999

It can't have been easy growing up as JFK Jr. Yes, he had a loving mother and sister, and the privileges that money can buy. But he also had to live his life in the glare of flashbulbs and, what must be equally annoying, in the heat of expectation. *Will he live up to the name? Will he carry on the tradition?* It's up to his enormous credit that he made his own life rather than trying to somehow echo his father's. He was his own man. Not the least of the sad ironies of this tragedy is that now, in the public reaction, he will be gathered back into the clan. His life will be seen as part of the Kennedy melodrama, and his loss part of the Kennedy curse.

—KENNETH AUCHINCLOSS, *Newsweek*, July 26, 1999

He attained a princely status not so much by birth but by bearing.

—SENATOR JOSEPH LIEBERMAN (D-CT)

He certainly had it. He had that charisma, that Kennedy charisma that all the Nixon people deeply resented and envied. He could have been quite a candidate.

—WILLIAM SAFIRE on *Meet the Press*, July 18, 1999

He was the tangible link to the magic of his father's White House Camelot— a simpler time when leaders were larger than life, when people dared to believe, when it seemed dreams were possible. With the crash of John-John's plane, we face the reality the link may be broken, forever, and so we pray for the Kennedy families. And for that little piece of our own dreams, as well.

—From an editorial in Ireland's *Calgary Sun*

It is rightfully said that the pictures of John-John gamboling under his father's desk in the Oval Office and bravely saluting the funeral cortege are our collective home movies. Seeing these images repeatedly on television this week was a reminder of the lost innocence of an age that abruptly ended on Nov. 22, 1963.

—WALTER SHAPIRO, *USA Today*, July 21, 1999

That little boy became a man who, for all his ease, was also a link to deep scars on the American political psyche. Indeed, that somber linkage made more striking the sunny and mannerly way he bore his celebrity when the cameras were tracking the days of his life rather than the way of his death.

—From an editorial in the *New York Times*, July 25, 1999

Senator Edward M. Kennedy's Eulogy for His Nephew, John F. Kennedy Jr.

Thank you, President and Mrs. Clinton and Chelsea, for being here today. You've shown extraordinary kindness through the course of this week.

Once, when they asked John what he would do if he went into politics and was elected president, he said, "I guess the first thing is call up Uncle Teddy and gloat." I loved that. It was so like his father.

From the first day of his life, John seemed to belong not only to our family, but to the American family.

The whole world knew his name before he did.

A famous photograph showed John racing across the lawn as his father landed in the White House helicopter and swept up John in his arms. When my brother saw that photo, he exclaimed, "Every mother in the United States is saying, 'Isn't it wonderful to see that love between a son and his father, the way that John races to be with his father.' Little do they know, that son would have raced right by his father to get to that helicopter."

But John was so much more than those long ago images emblazoned in our minds. He was a boy who grew into a man with a zest for life and a love of adventure. He was a pied piper who brought us all along. He was blessed with a father and mother who never thought anything mattered more than their children.

When they left the White House, Jackie's soft and gentle voice and unbreakable strength of spirit guided him surely and securely to the future. He had a legacy, and he learned to treasure it. He was part of a legend, and he learned to live with it. Above all, Jackie gave him a place to be himself, to grow up, to laugh and cry, to dream and strive on his own.

John learned that lesson well. He had amazing grace. He accepted who he was, but he cared more about what he could and should become. He saw things that could be lost in the glare of the spotlight. And he could laugh at the absurdity of too much pomp and circumstance.

He loved to travel across the city by subway, bicycle, and roller blade. He lived as if he were unrecognizable, although he was known by everyone he encountered. He always introduced himself, rather than take anything for granted. He drove his own car and flew his own plane, which is how he wanted it. He was the king of his domain.

He thought politics should be an integral part of our popular culture, and that popular culture should be an integral part of politics. He transformed that belief into the creation of *George*. John shaped and honed a fresh, often irreverent journal. His new political magazine attracted a new generation, many of whom had never read about politics before.

John also brought to *George* a wit that was quick and sure. The premier issue of *George* caused a stir with a cover photograph of Cindy Crawford dressed as George Washington with a bare belly button. The "Reliable Source" in the *Washington Post* printed a mock cover of *George* showing not Cindy Crawford, but me dressed as George Washington, with my belly button exposed. I suggested to John that perhaps I should have been the model for the first cover of his magazine. Without missing a beat, John told me that he stood by his original editorial decision.

John brought this same playful wit to other aspects of his life. He campaigned for me during my 1994 election and always caused a stir when he arrived in Massachusetts. Before one of his trips to Boston, John told the campaign he was bringing along a companion, but would need only one hotel room.

Interested, but discreet, a senior campaign worker picked John up at the airport and prepared to handle any media barrage that might accompany John's arrival with his mystery companion. John landed with the companion all right —an enormous German shepherd dog named Sam he had just rescued from the pound.

He loved to talk about the expression on the campaign worker's face and the reaction of the clerk at the Charles Hotel when John and Sam checked in.

I think now not only of these wonderful adventures, but of the kind of person John was. He was the son who quietly gave extraordinary time and ideas to the Institute of Politics at Harvard that bears his father's name. He brought to the Institute his distinctive insight that politics could have a broader appeal, that it was not just about elections, but about the larger forces that shape our whole society.

John was also the son who was once protected by his mother. He went on to become her pride—and then her protector in her final days. He was the Kennedy who loved us all, but who especially cherished his sister Caroline, celebrated her brilliance, and took strength and joy from their lifelong mutual admiration society.

And for a thousand days, he was a husband who adored the wife who became his perfect soul mate. John's father taught us all to reach for the moon and the stars. John did that in all he did—and he found his shining star when he married Carolyn Bessette.

How often our family will think of the two of them, cuddling affectionately on a boat, surrounded by family—aunts, uncles, Caroline and Ed and their children, Rose, Tatania, and Jack, Kennedy cousins, Radziwill cousins, Shriver cousins, Smith cousins, Lawford cousins—as we sailed Nantucket Sound.

Then we would come home, and before dinner, on the lawn where his father had played, John would lead a spirited game of touch football. And his beautiful young wife, the new pride of the Kennedys, would cheer for John's team and delight her nieces and nephews with her somersaults.

We loved Carolyn. She and her sister Lauren were young extraordinary women of high accomplishment—and their own limitless possibilities. We mourn their loss and honor their lives. The Bessette and Freeman families will always be part of ours.

John was a serious man who brightened our lives with his smile and his grace. He was a son of privilege who founded a program called Reaching Up to train better caregivers for the mentally disabled.

He joined Wall Street executives on the Robin Hood Foundation to help the city's impoverished children. And he did it all so quietly, without ever calling attention to himself.

John was one of Jackie's two miracles. He was still becoming the person he would be, and doing it by the beat of his own drummer. He had only just begun. There was in him a great promise of things to come.

The Irish Ambassador recited a poem to John's father and mother soon after John was born. I can hear it again now, at this different and difficult moment:

> We wish to the new child,
> A heart that can be beguiled,
> By a flower,
> That the wind lifts,
> As it passes.

If the storms break for him,
May the trees shake for him,
Their blossoms down.

In the night that he is troubled,
May a friend wake for him,
So that his time be doubled,
And at the end of all loving and love
May the Man above,
Give him a crown.

We thank the millions who have rained blossoms down on John's memory. He and his bride have gone to be with his mother and father, where there will never be an end to love. He was lost on that troubled night, but we will always wake for him, so that his time, which was not doubled, but cut in half, will love forever in our memory, and in our beguiled and broken hearts.

We dared to think, in that other Irish phrase, that this John Kennedy would live to comb gray hair, with his beloved Carolyn by his side. But like his father, he had every gift but length of years.

We who have loved him from the day he was born, and watched the remarkable man he became, now bid him farewell.

God bless you, John and Carolyn. We love you and we always will.

Many of the sources for this book are provided in the text. This section of source notes is also provided to amplify some of those references and are followed by a listing of the specific sources by name.

Chapter 1

Sources for this chapter included a wide range of Kennedy biographies (see bibliography) as well as extensive consultation of many other published sources, including newspapers and magazines going back over thirty years.

Chapter 2

Many of the details of John's early life were drawn from *White House Nannie*, as well as several other books about the Kennedy family; U.P.I., and Associated Press. The "John–John" story is from *Jacqueline Kennedy Onassis*. The Couri Hay anecdote is from *Prince Charming*. John's astrological profile was commissioned by the author; the numerological profile and graphology interpretation are author research. A wide range of books, newspapers and magazine articles (some of which are listed below) were consulted for the other details included in this chapter.

"One day Jack was . . " Lester David, *Jacqueline Kennedy Onassis: A Portrait of Her Private Years*, p. 152.

"Birth Force Number 7 . . .": Bernard Gittelson, *Intangible Evidence*, pp. 394–95.

"According to Gittelson . . .": Bernard Gittelson, *Intangible Evidence*, p. 515.

"John's writing climbs . . .": Bernard Gittelson, *Intangible Evidence*, p. 515.

"He also reveals . . .": Bernard Gittelson, *Intangible Evidence*, p. 520.

"This person . . .": Bernard Gittelson, *Intangible Evidence*, p. 524.

Chapter 3

Details on John's date with Meg Azozi were drawn from a photo in the August 16, 1993 issue of *People* magazine. Details on John's link to Audra Avizienis was also from *People* magazine. The Paula Barbieri section was drawn from *Day & Date*. Details on Carolyn Bessette were drawn from the *National Enquirer*, the *New York Post*, and other published sources. The Naomi Campbell anecdote was drawn from an article in *Cosmopolitan* magazine. The Princess Diana story was drawn from *People* and the *National Enquirer*. The Janice Dickinson material was drawn from the book, *Model*.

Details on John's links to Julie Baker, Jenny Christian, Christina Haag, Sally Munro, Sinead O'Connor, Julia Roberts, Stephanie Schmid, and Xuxa were drawn from *Prince Charming*. The section on John's date with Madonna was drawn from *Madonna Unauthorized* and *Prince Charming*, as well as several other published sources. The Elle MacPherson rumor first appeared in the British newspaper the *Sunday Mirror*. Other "romance" anecdotes were drawn from published sources, including those listed below.

"In a recent lengthy . . .": Wendy Leigh, *Prince Charming: The John F. Kennedy, Jr. Story*, pp. 196–97.

"It was untrue . . .": Wendy Leigh, *Prince Charming: The John F. Kennedy, Jr. Story*, pp. 304–5.

"Jackson beat Daryl . . .": Wendy Leigh, *Prince Charming: The John F. Kennedy, Jr. Story*, p. 305.

"Madonna biographer . . .": Christopher Andersen, *Madonna Unauthorized*, p. 267.

"Her only son . . .": Wendy Leigh, *Prince Charming: The John F. Kennedy, Jr. Story*, p. 257.

"Jackie warned him . . .": Christopher Andersen, *Madonna Unauthorized*, p. 268.

Chapter 4

Sources for this chapter included *Growing Up Kennedy*; *Jacqueline Kennedy Onassis*; *A Woman Named Jackie*; *The Kennedy Women*; *The Uncommon Wisdom of Jacqueline Kennedy Onassis*; *A Day in the Life of President Kennedy*; the *New York Post*; *Good Housekeeping*, and other published reports.

Chapter 5

Sources for this chapter included the *New York Times*; the *New Republic*; *Prince Charming*; *Time*; NBC; *People*; the *Today Show*; *Seinfeld*; *Murphy Brown*; and other published reports.

Chapter 6

The story of Shelby Shusteroff's nude photos of John is drawn from *Prince Charming*. Details on John's drinking and drug use were drawn from *A Woman Named Jackie*; *Prince Charming*; and other published sources. Details on the William Kennedy Smith trial were drawn from *The Kennedy Scandals & Tragedies*, live CNN coverage of the trial; *A Current Affair*; and other published sources. John's problems with the New York Bar exam were widely written about. Sources included *Newsweek*; the *New Republic*; the *New York Post*; the *New York Daily News*; *Prince Charming*; and other published sources. The "Brawl in the Park" was likewise widely covered by the media. Sources included *Day & Date*; *Hard Copy*; the *New York Post*; the *National Enquirer*; the *Howard Stern Show*; and several other published sources. The feature on the Jacqueline Kennedy Onassis auction was drawn from author research; Sotheby's and the Sotheby's catalog; *USA Today*; and *Larry King Live*.

"John seemed to develop . . .": Wendy Leigh, *Prince Charming: The John F. Kennedy, Jr. Story*, p. 191.

"Through 1983, John . . .": Wendy Leigh, *Prince Charming: The John F. Kennedy, Jr. Story*, p. 248.

"A Kennedy employee . . .": Wendy Leigh, *Prince Charming: The John F. Kennedy, Jr. Story*, p. 296.

Chapter 7

Sources for this chapter are provided in the text.

Chapter 8

Sources for this chapter are provided in the text.

Chapter 9

Sources for this chapter were the first five issues of *George* magazine.

Books

Andersen, Christopher. *Madonna Unauthorized*. New York: Simon & Schuster, 1991.

Bishop, Jim. *A Day in the Life of President Kennedy*. New York: Viking, 1961.

Bly, Nellie. *The Kennedy Men*. New York: Kensington Books, 1996.

Cameron, Gail. *Rose: A Biography of Rose Fitzgerald Kennedy*. New York: Berkley, 1971.

Collier, Peter and David Horowitz. *The Kennedys: An American Drama*. New York: Warner Books, 1984.

Current Biography, January 1996. New York: H. W. Wilson, 1996.

David, Lester. *Jacqueline Kennedy Onassis: A Portrait of Her Private Years* New Jersey: Birch Lane Press, 1994.

DeGregorio, William A. *The Complete Book of U.S. Presidents*. New York: Barricade Books, 1993.

Gittelson, Bernard. *Intangible Evidence*. New York: Simon & Schuster, 1987.

Gross, Michael. *Model: The Ugly Business of Beautiful Women*. New York: Warner Books, 1996.

Heymann, C. David. *A Woman Named Jackie: An Intimate Biography of Jacqueline Kennedy Onassis*. New York: Lyle Stuart, 1989.

James, Ann. *The Kennedy Scandals & Tragedies*. Lincolnwood, IL: Publications International, 1991.

Leamer, Laurence. *The Kennedy Women: The Saga of an American Family*. New York: Ivy Books, 1994.

Leigh, Wendy. *Prince Charming: The John F. Kennedy, Jr. Story*. New York: Signet, 1994.

Onassis, Jacqueline Kennedy. *The Uncommon Wit of Jacqueline Kennedy Onassis*. New Jersey: Citadel Press, 1996.

Rainie, Harrison and John Quinn. *Growing Up Kennedy: The Third Wave Comes of Age*. New York: Putnam, 1983.

Kennedy, Caroline and Ellen Alderman. *The Right to Privacy*. New York: Knopf, 1996.

Shaw, Maud. *White House Nannie: My Years with Caroline and John Kennedy, Jr*. New York: New American Library, 1996.

Sothebys. *The Estate of Jacqueline Kennedy Onassis* (auction catalog). New York, 1996.

Stone, Oliver. *JFK: The Book of the Film* New York: Applause Books, 1992.

Newspapers and Magazines

- *Cosmopolitan*
- *Elle*
- *Entertainment Weekly*
- *Esquire*
- *George*
- *Good Housekeeping*
- *GQ*
- *Ladies Home Journal*
- *Life*
- The *Los Angeles Times*
- *McCall's*
- The *National Enquirer*
- The *National Examiner*
- The *New Haven Register*
- The *New Republic*
- *New York*
- The *New Yorker*
- The *New York Daily News*
- The *New York Post*
- The *New York Times*
- *Newsweek*
- *People*
- *Playboy*
- The *Star*
- *Time*
- *TV Guide*
- *US*
- *U.S. News & World Report*
- *USA Today*
- *Vanity Fair*
- The *Wall Street Journal*
- The *Washington Post*

TV, Radio, Movies, and Documentaries

- ABC News
- Associated Press
- CBS News
- CNN
- *A Current Affair*
- *Day & Date*
- *Entertainment Tonight*
- *Four Days in November*
- *Good Morning America*
- *Hard Copy*
- The *Howard Stern Show*
- *Inside Edition*
- *Intimate Portraits: John F. Kennedy Jr.* (Lifetime)
- *JFK*
- *Larry King Live*
- *A Matter of Degrees*
- *Murphy Brown*
- NBC News
- *Prime Time Live*
- *Seinfeld*
- The *Today Show*
- UPI

Interviews

Journal Graphics; The author talked to several people who know John F. Kennedy Jr. personally and others who know people associated with him. These sources included childhood school friends, people who have been out with him socially, and others. All of these sources requested anonymity.

STEPHEN J. SPIGNESI specializes in popular culture subjects, including television, film, contemporary fiction, and historical biography. He has written several authorized entertainment books, working with Stephen King, Turner Entertainment, the Margaret Mitchell Estate, Andy Griffith, Viacom, and other personalities and entities on a wide range of projects.

His books include • *The Beatles Book of Lists* • *The Celebrity Baby Name Book* • *The Complete Stephen King Encyclopedia* • *The Complete Titanic* • *The "ER" Companion* • *The Gore Galore Video Quiz Book* • *The Hollywood Book of Lists* • *The Italian 100* • *The Lost Work of Stephen King* • *Mayberry, My Hometown* • *The Odd Index* • *The Official "Gone With the Wind" Companion* • *QVC's Consumer's Guide to Jewelry* • *The Robin Williams Scrapbook* • *The Stephen King Quiz Book* • *She Came in Through the Kitchen Window* • *The Second Stephen King Quiz Book* • *The U.F.O. Book of Lists* • *The V.C. Andrews Trivia and Quiz Book* • *What's Your "Friends" IQ?* • *What's Your "Mad About You" IQ?* • *The Woody Allen Companion.*

Spignesi has also contributed essays, chapters, and introductions to a wide range of books.

Spignesi's books have been translated into several languages, and he has also written for such publications as the *New York Times, Harper's*, the *New York Daily News,* and *Saturday Review.* He also appeared as a Kennedy authority in the 1998 E! documentary about the family.

In addition to his writing, Spignesi lectures on a variety of subjects and teaches writing in the Connecticut area. He is the founder and editor in chief of the small press publishing company, The Stephen John Press, which recently published the acclaimed feminist autobiography *Open Windows: The Autobiography of Charlotte Troutwine Braun.*

Spignesi is a graduate of the University of New Haven, and lives in new Haven with his wife, Pam.